THE CRYPTO ISLAND TAX GUIDE

CRYSTAL STRANGER, EA

Clear Advantage LLC
423 Kaiolu St. Unit 106
Honolulu, HI 96815

For information regarding special discounts for bulk purchases please
contact
Clear Advantage Special Sales at info@clearadvantage.com

Cover design by Katedra Hackett
Manufactured in the United States of America
1 2 3 4 5 6 7 8 9 10

Library of Congress Cataloging-in-Publication Data
Stranger, Crystal
The Crypto Island Tax Guide/
Crystal Stranger
p.cm.
Includes Index.

ISBN: 978-0578410074

CONTENTS

INTRODUCTION   Pg 5

CHAPTER 1   Pg 11
CRYPTO TAX ESSENTIALS

CHAPTER 2   Pg 37
CRYPTOCURRENCY AND OTHER INVESTMENTS

CHAPTER 3   Pg 49
DAOS AND MUTUAL FUNDS

CHAPTER 4   Pg 59
FOREIGN EARNED INCOME EXCLUSION

CHAPTER 5   Pg 71
FOREIGN TAX CREDIT

CHAPTER 6   Pg 79
TAX-FREE CRYPTO RETIREMENT SAVINGS

CHAPTER 7   Pg 87
BEACHSIDE RETIREMENT INCOME

CHAPTER 8   Pg 93
UNIVERSAL TAX DEDUCTIONS

CHAPTER 9   Pg 103
LAUNCHING AN INTERNATIONAL BUSINESS

CHAPTER 10   Pg 113
FOREIGN CORPORATIONS

CHAPTER 11   Pg 133
INITIAL COIN OFFERINGS

CHAPTER 12   Pg 139
NON-RESIDENT TAX ISSUES

CHAPTER 13   Pg 149
EXPATRIATION

CHAPTER 14   Pg 157
CRYPTO ASSET REPORTING REQUIREMENTS

CHAPTER 15   Pg 165
  GETTING CAUGHT UP
CHAPTER 16   Pg 175
  IRS PASSPORT REVOCATION
CHAPTER 17   Pg 181
  STATE TAX ISSUES
CHAPTER 18   Pg 121
  PRACTICALITIES
APPENDIX   Pg 225

INDEX   Pg 229

ACKNOWLEDGEMENTS

This book is dedicated to my husband, Andre Pattantyus, who has put up with all my crazy crypto investing schemes and ICO entrepreneurialism. Having a supportive partner and father for our children allowed me the freedom to make all this happen. And we met and got married on an island, so this is extra appropriate.

"AS CYBERCOMMERCE BEGINS, IT WILL LEAD INEVITABLY TO CYBERMONEY. THIS NEW FORM OF MONEY WILL RESET THE ODDS, REDUCING THE CAPACITY OF THE WORLD'S NATION-STATES TO DETERMINE WHO BECOMES A SOVEREIGN INDIVIDUAL."

-JAMES DALE DAVIDSON AND LORD WILLIAM REES MOOG, *THE SOVEREIGN INDIVIDUAL* (1997)

INTRODUCTION

Cryptocurrency has already changed the world in the decade Bitcoin has been in existence. No longer do central banks solely control the money supply, and the issuance of tokens has created a class of digital assets that can be traded across international borders. Many have already become wealthy from this new form of money and many new companies are popping up using the underlying technology of blockchain to create solutions to much of the world's problems.

Many of the entrepreneurs and traders who have become wealthy off of blockchain companies or trading cryptocurrencies have relocated to places like Puerto Rico that have favorable tax treatment for capital gains. Others are establishing citizenship abroad in plans of renouncing U.S. citizenship to no longer have to pay taxes on worldwide income. Still others are forming their companies in jurisdictions such as Malta, Switzerland, and Bermuda that offer a favorable legislative climate for promoting an initial coin offering (ICO).

The name of this book comes from the media calling the outposts of blockchain legislation "crypto islands." Many small countries and island nations have passed favorable legislation for ICOs as well as having good tax laws, with the goal of attracting these new technology companies to operate there and feed funds into the local economy. Not every country doing this has had the support of the local people, but this is always a challenge anywhere. Still, many people will find flexibility in their lives when it comes to making the best decisions on where to locate their business so that it can grow financially, which is shaping up to become a mass exodus of intelligence to idyllic locations the world over.

Living abroad is the dream of many American citizens, so this fits right in with this movement. Yet most Americans don't realize that their U.S. tax obligations remain wherever in the world they may live. Once I began working with expat clients, I was shocked at how little other tax professionals I would speak with knew about this subject. Few courses are available to the tax community on issues such as tax treaties or informational returns, let alone the general public. And in the blockchain space, the lack of knowledge and misunderstandings have been even more extreme.

My intention with writing this book is not to give you enough knowledge to prepare your return. That is impossible without creating a comprehensive textbook. What I want is to give you an overview of the many areas of U.S. taxation that you can both discover savings and avoid trouble, and to help bridge the communication gaps I often see between tax professionals and their clients.

Having worked with clients the world over, I have had the blessing of hearing multitudes of amazing stories of living in various cultures. And I have traveled extensively and lived abroad as well. I gave birth to my daughter while I was living in Norway. In addition to running my own firm, 1st Tax, on a contract basis, I worked for the last five years as a tax manager, supervising more than 2,000 tax returns per year at one of the largest expat tax firms in the world, Taxes For Expats. This has given me direct, personal knowledge of the workings of expat tax laws and how the aspects of living abroad relate to tax compliance. Many of these laws affect all cryptocurrency investors and blockchain businesses because cryptocurrency is not held in a single location, so in many cases it can be considered a foreign account or foreign income just by the nature of what it is.

Every day I run across new situations and learn additional nuances to apply to this area of work. Tax law is ever evolving in big and small ways alike. The Tax Cuts and Jobs Act (TCJA) passed at the end of 2017 made major changes to all areas of tax law. Most notable among them was an overhaul of international corporate taxation. We will touch on this in the later chapters and cover the changes to individual taxes, but to cover the foreign corporate taxes in any detail would make a long and dry book that nobody except another tax practitioner would even want to consider reading.

This book is as accurate and current as what I can now ascertain—but in six months, a year, who knows? Yet with the utter and complete lack of professional information available to the public on this subject, as well as a plethora of misleading, or downright incorrect, information online, I feel there is a great need for this material to be accessible to both the taxpaying public affected by these issues as well as the tax professional community. Therefore, I have decided to share my knowledge through this book in the hopes it will dispel some of the mistruths and incorrect assumptions I hear frequently.

Writing this book, I have tried to refrain from

getting into too much technical detail whenever possible. I don't want to alienate the average reader by writing a textbook-style book filled with endless paragraphs of barely comprehensible "legalese." Although I have recently been asked to work on a textbook covering these subjects in greater detail as well, so that may be one of the next projects to add to my "someday" list. I have also intentionally refrained from footnotes so as to make the reading more fluid. The appendix at the end has references that you can review if you are interested in having a more thorough understanding of the IRS materials and tax court cases that are the basis used for preparing this book.

I love this area of work because it is never boring. There are always new complexities and different situations that must be sifted. The financial puzzles and challenging legal definitions are what keep me coming back. Two days working with foreign taxation issues are never the same. I am also blessed in that working with international clients makes it very easy to work remotely, giving me the freedom to live and work from anywhere.

Let me express my gratitude for you picking up this book. I hope that my enthusiasm and fascination of the tax system will help inspire you to learn more and make the most informed decisions related to your own financial situation.

1. CRYPTO TAX ESSENTIALS

You've made a bundle of money from investing in cryptocurrencies and didn't think they were taxable income, now what? Perhaps you have been filing every year, but wonder if you have been meeting all the requirements correctly, or if you could save more in taxes. Or you may be a tax professional looking for a greater understanding of the complexities of cryptocurrency tax issues. Some readers of this book may also be deeper down the rabbit hole and have started companies using blockchain technology and wonder how the complex tax laws apply to them. As you can see, the audience this book is written for has many levels of involvement in the cryptocurrency world. Please be patient with me as I cover some basics. I want to make sure we're not leaving anyone behind, although this is complex material to learn.

While you may want to skip ahead if you know taxation concepts well, I've found in many conversations with supposed "experts" in this area of tax law, that they have vast misunderstandings of very basic topics. So I would suggest you give it all a read as a refresher if nothing else. The one exception to this is the state tax chapter at the end, which I have included more as reference material than anything else.

Understanding U.S. Tax Law

One of the great complications in our modern world with increased mobility and global economy is that every country has their own unique tax laws. With the 2017 Tax Cuts and Jobs Act, the United States has made a major shift in tax theory, changing from a worldwide system to a territorial system. The magnitude of changes this represents is not likely to be well understood for a decade or more.

Not only does the Tax Cuts and Jobs Act represent sweeping changes in many areas of taxation, but it was also a very hastily written treatise. The last major tax overhaul in 1986 took 18 months to write and pass the law, whereas the recent bill was passed in only seven weeks!

I was asked to submit comments on the first House of Representatives bill and the Brady Revision, and many of my comments surrounded the lack of clarity with the foreign provisions. Some of this was revised by the time it reached the Senate bill, but the Senate never opened their bill to tax professional organizations for comment.

There was a lot of pressure to pass the bill while the Republicans held a majority in both the House and Senate, and thus I doubt many senators even read the 1,097 pages of the bill—let alone understood it. Thus, I would expect there to be some Congressional updates over the next couple of years to correct many of the errors contained in the provisions of the original bill. The 1986 tax bill had a major correction voted through two years later, and we will likely see similar changes going forward with the 2017 package.

Whenever there is new tax law it is a mainly theoretical exercise to interpret it. This is because tax law is determined not just by Congress, but also by judicial interpretation of the Tax Court, Appeals Courts, and the Supreme Court. Until a new law has been proven through these courts, it is always a big question mark if it is even enforceable.

The international aspects of the new laws in particular have many potential legal challenges. It is not yet known if foreign countries will determine some of the tax law provisions to be in violation of trade agreements or tax treaties. Additionally, there may be conflicts with the Administrative Procedures Act (APA), as many of the prior laws that were passed with the intention of curbing inversions have proved unenforceable because of APA conflicts.

So what does this mean for you? I always give my clients the option of how aggressive they want to be. The risk, of course, is that the more aggressive you are, the more likely you are to get audited. Sometimes even if something is a winning position and technically legal, it is not worth pursuing because the savings would not justify the time and cost of defending the position if and when it was questioned.

You will need to discuss the law changes and how it affects you with your tax. If they don't treat you like you are intelligent, or don't meet with your risk profile, find a new advisor. And, above all, don't fall prey to the endless hucksters selling tax shelters, as they will cost you in the long run. Tax shelters with the main purpose of avoiding taxes are *never* legal.

What *is* legal? Planning to minimize taxes

while maximizing business or other financial advantages. Always keep in mind that any plan instituted strictly for tax aversion purposes will be disallowed in court. This is how most people get in trouble. It is a thin line, so it is wise to document your reasons for making changes and to avoid working with any company that markets complex plans for tax savings.

Now you should understand a little more about U.S. tax law. As such, it is time to delve into the intricacies of how U.S. tax law is applied around the world.

What is a Foreign Country?

If you have abroad for a while, the United States likely feels like a foreign country, as where you live is home, so calling your country of residence "foreign" can feel awkward, right? I find many individuals struggle just with the terminology involved in this U.S. tax process, so one of the first items that need to be clarified is what the IRS determines to be a foreign country. Once this is defined, I will stick with using "foreign" as the term of description henceforth, as constantly adding the alternate terminology of "non-U.S." instead feels like it breaks up the stream of consciousness.

> For U.S. tax purposes, a foreign country is defined as any country other than the 50 states, U.S. possessions, or territories.

Simple, right? Does this mean then that if you live in a U.S. possession, such as the crypto-haven of Puerto Rico, that you do not need to file a Federal tax return? Possibly. Depends on the possession.

There are five inhabited U.S. possessions: Puerto Rico, the U.S. Virgin Islands, Guam, American Samoa, and the Commonwealth of the Northern Mariana Islands. Only in the Northern Marianas and U.S. Virgin Islands are bona fide residents generally not required to file a U.S. resident income tax return. For the other locations, U.S. income tax returns usually must be filed, but few will owe tax. Income generally in these locations is treated as exempt from U.S. tax if the taxpayer is a bona fide resident, and if not a bona fide resident, all income is subject to U.S. tax with a foreign tax credit available for taxes paid to the possession.

That got a bit technical, as tax definitions tend to do. If you don't understand a concept, please read on, as the answer to your question is likely covered in later material. Bona fide residents will be defined clearly in the next chapter, and foreign tax credits will be discussed in chapter 3.

Contrary to popular belief, possession of a U.S. passport does not mean that the holder is a U.S. citizen. Some possessions, such as the Northern Marianas, allow a resident to adopt U.S. nationality, thus being issued a U.S. passport without taking on U.S. citizenship. Taxpayers in this situation would file as a non-resident, unless meeting the actual residency rules as defined in the substantial presence test. For more information, please see Chapter 12 about Non-Resident Tax returns for a full explanation of the substantial presence test.

New Restrictions

Starting in March 2010, it became a more difficult world for Americans living abroad with the passing of the Foreign Account Tax Compliance Act, also known as FATCA. This is one of the areas I would suspect most cryptocurrency investors are least knowledgable, as many tax professionals do not understand how to correctly report non-U.S. financial accounts, or when these accounts need to be reported. The added pressure on foreign banks to report U.S. citizens has caused many foreign banks to refrain from issuing bank accounts to U.S. citizens. I have also had many clients for whom U.S. banks have refused to issue new accounts or closed accounts of U.S. citizens living abroad. This should come as no surprise to those in the crypto world, where being denied bank accounts or having them revoked because of cryptocurrency holdings is not uncommon.

The Burden of U.S. Citizenship

Everyone born in the United States or with parents who are U.S. citizens and meet certain residency requirements acquires U.S. citizenship at birth. This has now become an issue for many people who acquired U.S. citizenship at birth but never realized this made them subject to U.S. tax laws.

Citizenship by Birth

Every person born on U.S. soil automatically acquires U.S. citizenship at birth. Many people born outside of the United States to parents who are U.S. citizens also acquire citizenship at birth. Unlike in many countries, you do not need to apply for your U.S. citizenship. This is automatically granted, and the application process is merely a technicality to obtain paperwork such as a passport or Social Security card.

While this is a blessing for many people, and is the cornerstone of our country being the "cultural melting pot" of the world, it also causes many problems. With the FATCA bank restrictions, many people have been surprised to be informed by their bankers that they are subject to U.S. tax laws. I know of several cases where a person had been born stateside yet lived their entire life outside the United States, and because of this, had the banks freeze their accounts. Their banks saw the U.S. birth location and demanded that they show documentation of compliance with all federal tax and informational return reporting requirements. Of course, they did not have this information handy, as they had not been aware they were U.S. citizens in the first place. These individuals had to become current with their tax requirements for five years before they could even renounce citizenship.

Dual Citizens

Lucky you to have citizenship in more than one country and the ease of working in the global economy. Poor you for having U.S. citizenship that will tax your worldwide income until the day you die —and then beyond the grave.

Double taxation is the name of the game. Despite many documents like tax treaties created with the intention of eliminating this, the reality is double taxation is likely here for the long haul. The problem lies in the concept of fiscal residency choice or, rather, that there are limited options available to be able to select your country of residence. The "closer-ties" rules will be the determining factor as to which country you pay the most tax. Even then, you likely will need to still file and pay in the other country in addition to filing in the United States.

I can personally attest to the increasing trend in recent years of U.S. citizens renouncing their citizenship in light of FATCA and the restrictive worldwide income aspects of U.S. tax law. I have also known many people who wanted U.S. citizenship. One must take into consideration that their children may wish to have U.S. citizenship to be able to easily live and work in the U.S. someday, as U.S. work visas are quite challenging to obtain. This alone can be enough to warrant retaining citizenship, but that is a very individual decision to make.

Filing Status

You have more options if you are married to a non-resident alien and live outside the United States. If your spouse has no income, you can elect to have him or her included on your return as a joint filer, and apply for your spouse's ITIN number. But if your spouse's income is as or more than yours, it most likely will benefit you to file separately. Once you make this election you can't easily go back. You must continue to file married filing joint annually. This isn't something you can decide on a year-to-year basis. This election must be made with a statement attached to your tax return.

The IRS offers these seven facts to help you choose the best filing status for you:

1 **Marital Status.** Your marital status on the last day of the year is your marital status for the entire year.
2 **If You Have a Choice.** If more than one filing status fits you, choose the one that allows you to pay the lowest taxes.
3 **Single Filing Status.** Single filing status generally applies if you are not married, divorced or legally separated according to state law.
4 **Married Filing Jointly.** A married couple may file a return together using the Married Filing Jointly status. If your spouse died during 2012, you usually may still file a joint return for that year.
5 **Married Filing Separately.** If a married couple decides to file their returns separately, each person's filing status would generally be Married Filing Separately.
6 **Head of Household.** The Head of Household status generally applies if you are not married and have paid more than half the cost of maintaining a home for yourself and a qualifying person.
7 **Qualifying Widow(er) with Dependent Child.** This status may apply if your spouse died during 2010 or 2011, you have a dependent child and you meet certain other conditions.

From: https://www.irs.gov/uac/Newsroom/Determining-Your-Correct-Filing-Status

If needed, applying for an ITIN for a spouse or child is a relatively simple process. You complete Form W-7 and attach this to your return, then mail the tax return with the W-7 to a special address for processing, unless the application is part of a Streamlined Procedure filing, which I will cover later in chapter 15. The biggest roadblock to this is normally obtaining the certified copy of your passport to mail in, as this must be certified by the passport office that issues this, i.e., directly by the government agency that issued the document, and not by a notary public or U.S. Embassy.

If you have children and are married to a non-resident alien, you are able to choose "Head of Household" filing status, even if you have not obtained Social Security numbers for these children. This contradicts the basic rule of Head of Household status that you must not live with your spouse for at least half the year to claim this. However, if you are married to a non-resident alien spouse, you are considered "unmarried" for purposes of claiming Head of Household. This does not carry over to other areas though, and this "unmarried" designation does not mean you can file as "Single." Your choices are "Married Filing Separately," "Head of Household with Qualifying Child," or "Married Filing Jointly," which I will cover next. To be able to be used as a child for Head of Household filing status, the child must meet the IRS's definition of a Qualifying Child.

Per the IRS, to be a taxpayer's qualifying child, a person must satisfy four tests:

- **Relationship** — the taxpayer's child or stepchild (whether by blood or adoption), foster child, sibling or step-sibling, or a descendant of one of these.
- **Residence** — has the same principal residence as the taxpayer for more than half the tax year. Exceptions apply, in certain cases, for children of divorced or separated parents, kidnapped children, temporary absences, and for children who were born or died during the year.
- **Age** — must be under the age of 19 at the end of the tax year, or under the age of 24 if a full-time student for at least five months of the year, or be permanently and totally disabled at any time during the year.
- **Support** — did not provide more than one-half of his/her own support for the year.

If your children are U.S. citizens, however, it is recommended to obtain Social Security numbers for them, as then you will also be able to make use of other tax advantages related to children such as dependency exemption, child care credit, and education credits. The Child Tax Credit used to offer a large advantage to many taxpayers, but the ability to claim this for non-U.S. residents was closed in early 2015 and will no longer be available to anyone living outside the United States for tax years 2015 and forward, or in past years for most circumstances, as new IRS regulations on this just came out and they have applied this to prior years as well.

If you realize while reading this that perhaps you could have claimed a more advantageous filing status on a previous year's return, you may be in luck. You have the opportunity to amend your return for filing status changes for three years following the due date of the original returns that were filed. This does not include any extensions however; it is restricted to the standard April 15 filing date of the year in question.

Gay Marriage

The June 2015 Supreme Court case granting legal marital status to those in same-sex marriages was a landmark case heralded by many. And despite the IRS already having acknowledged the need for regulation on this front—especially with regard to state-level status—there was a new series of complications for married same-sex taxpayers who now had to file jointly. This case was especially pertinent to those same-sex couples living abroad in countries where same-sex marriage is not recognized.

For example, a same-sex couple who are living in Switzerland and were married in Belgium would have the option of filing either as Single or as Married Filing Separate. This is because in Switzerland they would be considered unmarried, so logically, continuing this tax pattern with a U.S. return is allowable, and would keep everything consistent and easy to follow. This would also allow the U.S. taxpayer to be able to e-file the tax return, which gives the convenience of annual filing. The other option would be to recognize the marriage and file either as married filing separately, or apply for an ITIN number to file jointly with the non-resident alien spouse. This has advantages in that if the U.S. taxpayer has significant assets, they will then be able to pass these on to their spouse upon death under the unlimited spousal exemption. But unless they have an estate that exceeds the current estate tax exemption, this is a worthless exercise.

Non-Residents

As I mentioned at the beginning of this chapter, some of you may be non-residents who earn U.S. source income. In this case, you will need to file Form 1040NR and only report your U.S.-based income. If you have spent too much time in the United States over the past three years, however, that will not be an option. Later in this book there is a chapter devoted to the intricacies of non-resident tax issues, although this really could be a whole other book.

First Year of Residency

For non-residents, the first year you are considered a

resident generally starts when you meet the substantial presence test. If you are a U.S. resident starting only in the current calendar year and were not a U.S. resident in the prior year, however, then the date of residence starts when you first arrive in the United States. For green card holders it is the first day you enter U.S. soil in possession of your green card.

When to File

The IRS has been generous in granting additional time to file for those who live abroad; the general extension being applied automatically for a June 15 filing date. Yet this does not give additional time to pay any taxes owed, which must be done by April 15 or interest and penalties will accrue. Therefore, if you think you may owe money, it is best to file prior to April 15. Also, non-resident taxpayers who are required to file Form 1040NR must file tax returns or extensions by April 15, regardless of where in the world they are living.

You can file an extension prior to June 15 that will give you until October 15 to complete filing. Under certain circumstances you can obtain a longer extension. One of these is to qualify for the Bona Fide Resident Test for the Foreign Earned Income Exclusion. In order to receive this extension, you must file Form 2350 and it must be received by the

IRS before October 15.

An additional two-month general extension for foreign residents can also be requested until December 15. There is no form for this, however. To apply, you will need to mail a letter to the IRS explaining the circumstances and making the request. As with Form 2350, a postmark before the cut-off date isn't enough; it has to be in the physical possession of the IRS by October 15 to be valid. This is not an automatic extension; it is up to the discretion of the IRS.

Civilian contractors working in U.S. military zones qualify for an extension of time not only to file their taxes but to pay their taxes as well. This extension covers the full period of service, plus an additional 180-day period after returning home.

Combat zones are designated by an Executive Order from the President as areas in which the U.S. Armed Forces are engaging or have engaged in combat. There are currently three such combat zones (including the airspace above each):

- Arabian Peninsula Areas, beginning Jan. 17, 1991 -- the Persian Gulf, Red Sea, Gulf of Oman, the part of the Arabian Sea north of 10° North latitude and west of 68° East longitude, the Gulf of Aden, and the countries of Bahrain, Iraq, Kuwait, Oman, Qatar, Saudi Arabia and the United Arab Emirates.
- Kosovo area, beginning Mar. 24, 1999 -- Federal Republic of Yugoslavia (Serbia and Montenegro), Albania, the Adriatic Sea and the Ionian Sea north of the 39th Parallel.
- Afghanistan, beginning Sept. 19, 2001.

Public Law 104-117 designates three parts of the former Yugoslavia as a Qualified Hazardous U.S. Duty Area, to be treated as if it were a combat zone, beginning Nov. 21, 1995 -- Bosnia and Herzegovina, Croatia, and Macedonia.

In addition, the Department of Defense has certified these locations for combat zone tax benefits due to their direct support of military operations, beginning on the listed dates:

In support of Operation Enduring Freedom (Afghanistan combat zone):

- Pakistan, Tajikistan and Jordan - Sept. 19, 2001
- Incirlik Air Base, Turkey - Sept. 21, 2001 through Dec. 31, 2005
- Kyrgyzstan and Uzbekistan - Oct. 1, 2001
- Philippines (only troops with orders referencing Operation Enduring Freedom) - Jan. 9, 2002
- Yemen - Apr. 10, 2002
- Djibouti - July 1, 2002
- Israel - Jan. 1 through July 31, 2003
- Somalia - Jan. 1, 2004

In support of Operation Iraqi Freedom (Arabian Peninsula Areas combat zone):

- Turkey - Jan. 1, 2003 through Dec. 31, 2005
- the Mediterranean Sea east of 30° East longitude - Mar. 19 through July 31, 2003
- Jordan - Mar. 19, 2003
- Egypt - Mar. 19 through Apr. 20, 2003

What Is Foreign Income?

The first questions clients ask about taxes usually involve what income must be reported. For U.S.

citizens or green card holders, this means all income earned worldwide, with very specific exceptions. For those who have other types of visas, generally just U.S. income is required to be reported if you are able to file as a non-resident. But if you fall under the qualifications of a being treated as a resident, then you must report *all* worldwide income.

Calculating wage income for U.S. taxes when living as an expat can be a bit complex. Many items must be included for income that would not be an issue in the United States and, contrarily, other items are excluded.

Employer contributions to pension funds must be included for residents of the majority of countries, but there are a few exceptions. Four countries—Belgium, Germany, Netherlands, and the United Kingdom—have pension plans that are defined as "qualified plans" by the IRS, meaning they are treated similar to a US 401(k) and do not need to be included as income. Since these four countries also have high tax rates, however, you have the option of including the pension funds as income in these countries, then including the income on Form 1116. This will allow you to have the contributions later become a basis for keeping a portion of the retirement distributions not taxable. Taxability of distributions from foreign pension funds are calculated in the same way as traditional IRA accounts with after-tax contributions. In addition, including employer contributions as income will allow you to accumulate a foreign tax credit carryover. Once a pattern of the most beneficial way of doing this is determined, the filing should be maintained and the pension contribution should be treated the same way in following years. Treatment should not be switched from year to year, or it will become nearly impossible to track the non-taxable basis down the line, when you receive retirement income.

There are some exceptions in other countries as well, but they are few and far between, and much less well defined. The main point I want to bring across is that, in general, it is wise to report these accounts. But if you are in a situation where your U.S. tax is high, there may be alternatives available if you keep looking.

It is important to note that employer pension contributions are not considered income for Foreign Earned Income Exclusion purposes, and must be removed for that calculation. Nonetheless they are considered earned income for foreign tax credit in the general category. Confusing, right? Don't worry, I will cover this in more detail in chapters to come.

Housing reimbursement must also be included as income in most cases. Government employees should not report this income, as the Living Quarters Allowance is considered non-taxable income as it is treated as a reimbursement rather than a fringe benefit. Government contractors must still report this as income, however.

PAYE System

Many countries have adopted a system where the majority of residents do not need to file tax returns. Tax is withheld from a worker's wages, then at the end of the year the government sends a prepared tax return. At that point you have the opportunity to agree or disagree with the results. This is quite opposite from the U.S. system that requires everyone above certain income levels to file a tax return each year.

There can be some confusion when preparing a U.S. return based off the information provided by countries with a PAYE system. Oftentimes there is income that is not taxable in that country but will be taxable in the United States, and the information for this taxable income can be challenging to find.

Self-Employment

In the United States, if you earn more than $400 a year from self-employment or work as an independent contractor, you must file a tax return. This is different than many countries, which have much higher thresholds for when returns need to be filed by entrepreneurs.

Expats who are self-employed run a much higher risk of audit. Therefore you must be very careful that your expenses are reasonable. It is good to try and imagine if each cost would meet the "ordinary and necessary" criteria that the IRS would use to judge your expenses under examination. Reading tax court cases is one of the best ways to get an idea of this, and also where a good tax advisor earns their worth.

International Organizations

Certain international organizations such as the United Nations (UN) or World Health Organization (WHO) are excluded from paying Social Security taxes in the United States. This does not mean these payments are exempt from income tax. If the amounts are fully excluded by the Foreign Earned Income Exclusion, then they will be tax free, but income above the exclusion amounts are still taxable.

Many employees of international organizations mistakenly believe their income is fully tax exempt. However, this is incorrect. What the WHO is referring to when they talk about the tax treaty exclusion of their workers' income is the exclusion from the Social Security tax for income earned outside the United States. If you are issued a U.S.

Form 1099 from an international organization, this should not be reported on Schedule C like other 1099s. Instead, this income should be reported directly on the Form 1040, and the self-employment (SE) tax exemption processed in the same manner used for tax treaty countries, including an explanatory statement.

International organizations often have life and health insurance plans that are considered fully qualified, meaning that amounts paid for these benefits do not need to be included in gross wages. In addition, their pension funds are considered IRS-qualified. This means they should be treated similarly to a domestic 401k plan, where the amounts contributed by employer and employee alike are not considered gross income. Also, the earnings in these retirement accounts are considered tax deferred.

Scholarships and Fellowships

Foreign scholarships, fellowships, research stipends, and grants are all considered income for Foreign Earned Income Exclusion and IRA contribution purposes. When from non-U.S. sources, these payments must be considered wages and cannot be reported on Schedule C as self-employment income. If from U.S. sources, however, scholarships and fellowships are only considered income for these purposes if shown in box 1 of Form W-2, or listed on a 1099-MISC and thus reported as self-employment income.

In general, when used for tuition, fees, books and necessary equipment, funds from scholarships and fellowships are not taxable and do not need to be reported as income. However, certain expenses related to fellowships and grants must be included in gross income, including:

- Amounts spent on room and board, travel, or optional equipment.

- Amounts received for teaching, research, or other services performed in order to receive the grant.

Community Property Countries

Countries including France, Germany, Italy, Switzerland, and South Africa have rules that define marital property as shared equally by a couple after marriage. This means that a spouse's income should be 50% taken into consideration when filing tax returns as married filing separately. For earned income, such as wages or business income, this is not practicable. It should also be noted that these laws are not applied in the same way community property laws are applied for states.

How this is applied on an international level is that, in community property countries, for any unearned income from accounts that are jointly owned with an non-resident alien spouse, 100% of the income from that account should be included. For example, if you own a bank account jointly with your spouse and it earns $50 in interest, if you live in Brazil you will only report $25 worth of interest on your tax return, whereas if you live in Switzerland you will need to report the full $50.

Students

Scholarships, fellowships, and other school income can be confusing as to taxability, even within the United States. When studying overseas, it can be quite challenging to determine what constitutes income. In general, scholarships are not taxable to the extent that they are spent directly on educational costs such as tuition, fees, and books. Income used for housing and other living expenses would be taxable and must be included in wages.

Fellowships, scholarships, grants, research stipends, and other awards are all considered wages and excludable with the Foreign Earned Income Exclusion. Still, you must include in gross income all amounts paid for incidental expenses, such as travel or room and board.

2. CRYPTOCURRENCY AND OTHER INVESTMENTS

Cryptocurrencies have proven to be a worthy investment for many. But properly reporting this on taxes can be daunting to say the least. There are several issues to contend with regarding investment income that are far more complex for cryptocurrency investors than for others, including the classification of what type of investment you have, which is not always clear at first glance. We will start with the meat of reporting cryptocurrency transactions, then get into how to report other types of common investment income.

Cryptocurrency

John McAfee frequently tells crowds at conferences not to pay their taxes and that the government has no right to tax your cryptocurrency funds, but this is simply not true. Your earnings on cryptocurrency are taxable: The problem is in telling what actually is earnings and determining what kind of income it really is.

One issue is that cryptocurrency has been determined by the IRS to be a property and not a currency. This is an important distinction because it means that every payment made in cryptocurrency is a taxable transaction that must be reported as a capital gain or loss. This means if you bought the famous Bitcoin pizza many years ago that would be worth millions now, you would have had to pay tax based on the value at the time you bought the pizza. Gratefully, at least the tax isn't based on the current value.

Still, this is a hard concept for many people to understand. If you go to a store that accepts Bitcoin for payment and spend the equivalent of $20 in Bitcoin on a sweater, then when tax time rolls around the next year you need to report that $20 spent as income. Of course, you wouldn't necessarily pay tax on the full $20. The tax owed would be the difference between $20 and what you had paid to buy that Bitcoin originally. So if you had bought the Bitcoin back in 2011 you probably would pay tax on nearly the full $20, but if you bought the Bitcoin in mid-2017 when it was worth double what it is now, you would report a cost basis of $40, and you would report a $20 loss on your taxes that can be used to offset other income.

This is the basic cryptocurrency tax concept that I would imagine many people have missed. But it isn't always so simple. The classification process still is highly debated between government agencies. The SEC considers most of the tokens issued to be securities, but they consider Bitcoin to not be a security. Well then, does this mean it could be argued that Bitcoin is actually a currency? Only time will tell if this argument can be successfully defended.

Additionally, there are other potential classifications that some tokens could fall under. Tokenized venture funds could be considered Passive Foreign Investment Companies (PFICs), as discussed further in chapter 5. Thus you must be careful to not jump to the conclusion that all cryptocurrency investments are treated as property for capital gains.

Interest

Interest paid on bank accounts the world over are

considered U.S. income. With loans made in cryptocurrencies it is not this simple, as interest if made in a cryptocurrency would not necessarily be considered interest under U.S. law. Instead, it would be reported as a capital gain of property when received.

This treatment of cryptocurrency interest actually could be better for many cryptocurrency investors, as capital losses may be used to offset against this income. If you are the borrower, however, and making interest payments in cryptocurrency, this could count against you as the interest would not be a deductible expense for U.S. taxes. Most of the cryptocurrency loan products I have seen, though, use the cryptocurrency as collateral and the loans are marked in fiat currency such as U.S. dollars or euros. But this is important to note as the industry is still developing and products with loans made in cryptocurrency are likely to come soon.

If you do pay interest in a fiat currency, any amount of interest earned over $20 is required to be reported. Even if you earn less than $20, it is still recommended you report any gains, as it helps relieve any IRS doubts about hiding income. If you have a joint account with your non-resident alien spouse, you must also report the interest on this account as your income. This messes up a lot of people, as they don't always realize this is income since the funds are not on their account.

Tax Tip: remember to report all worldwide income and bank accounts. If you are added to an account of a family member abroad, this likely will create taxable income for you.

Especially if you report large bank account balances on the FBAR report or Form 8938, it is expected by the IRS that you will show income earned. This is not always the case however, as in some parts of the world bank accounts do not earn interest because of local laws. This is common in Middle Eastern countries where Islamic banking practices are prevalent. The lack of earned interest is likely to be questioned by the IRS at some point, so be prepared by having your statements showing the balances available.

Stocks

For any U.S. person, meaning citizens, green card holders, or U.S. residents, capital gains on any investments sold worldwide are treated like domestic gains, with the exception of residents of Puerto Rico who are taxed under Puerto Rico law rather than U.S. law. This is based on gains over when you initially purchased the property, even if you were not a citizen at that time. This can be a hidden issue involved with including a non-resident alien spouse on a tax return. For example, if you purchased stock in XYZ company in 2002 at $10 a share, became a U.S. resident in 2015 and sell the stock for $50, you will pay tax on the full capital gains of $40 per share. Because of this situation, it may be more beneficial to sell investments you own in the year prior to becoming a U.S. person.

> Tax Tip:
>
> Sell stocks or other investments with stepped up gain in the year before becoming a U.S. resident or before treating your non-resident alien spouse as a resident on your tax return to avoid big capital gains hits.

Security Token Offerings (STOs) are becoming more common as fundraising tools. As these offerings are structured similar to standard securities, it is likely the treatment will be the same as stocks, but this is still to be determined and may change when we finally have regulation.

Qualified Dividends

Foreign dividends paid from treaty countries are considered qualified dividends, as are dividends from any company registered on the U.S. stock exchange and held for certain holding periods. No payments from cryptocurrency investments right now would be considered qualified dividends, which can be a real tax disadvantage of tokenized securities.

Dividends received from Passive Foreign Investment Companies such as foreign mutual funds are never considered qualified dividends, even in treaty countries. This makes perfect sense, as it would be nearly impossible to determine the holding period to meet the qualifications. How would you know if the investments were in a treaty country even if the country where the fund is based qualifies? They may have investments as part of the fund in companies all over the world.

Countries with Qualified Dividends:

Australia	India	Pakistan
Austria	Indonesia	Philippines
Bangladesh	Ireland	Poland
Barbados	Israel	Portugal
Belgium	Italy	Romania
Bulgaria	Jamaica	Russian Federation
Canada	Japan	Slovak Republic
China	Kazakhstan	South Africa
Cyprus	Korea	Spain
Czech Republic	Latvia	Sri Lanka
Denmark	Lithuania	Sweden
Egypt	Slovenia	Switzerland
Estonia	Luxembourg	Thailand
Finland	Malta	Trinidad and Tobago
France	Mexico	Tunisia
Germany	Morocco	Turkey
Greece	Netherlands	Ukraine
Hungary	New Zealand	United Kingdom
Iceland	Norway	Venezuela

It is more arguable whether earnings from STOs could be considered qualified dividends when distributed. If the distributions are called dividends, it would seem that they could be considered qualified. However, certain other structures such as master limited partnerships and real estate investment trusts are specifically excluded from qualified dividend status. If STOs are excluded as well, this could become a major disadvantage tax-wise for investing in tokenized securities compared to traditional stocks.

Real Estate

Rental real estate is one of the best long-term investments the world over. For U.S. citizens buying rental property abroad, most of the same U.S. laws will apply to owning property here.

One notable exception is how depreciation is handled. Property owned within the United States is given an accelerated depreciation period of 27.5 years for residential rental property. For residential rental homes owned outside the United States, though, a recovery period of 40 years must be used instead.

Earnings in Pension Accounts

For taxpayers who are highly compensated individuals, earnings of monies held in pension accounts are taxable annually. According to the IRS, those who earn more than $120,000 per year are considered highly compensated individuals. For some countries there are treaty exclusions available in order for this to not be currently taxable, but not every country has a treaty with the United States for this.

Net Investment Income Tax

The Affordable Care Act introduced a provision to help raise funds for health care by implementing the Net Investment Income Tax (NIIT), a 3.8% tax on passive income for certain taxpayers. This can have big impact on cryptocurrency investors living abroad because this tax comes in after credits are taken out, so even if you have a large foreign tax credit, this will not offset NIIT tax.

Income Threshold for NIIT:

Filing Status:	Threshold Amount:
Married Filing Jointly	$250,000
Married Filing Separately	$125,000
Single	$200,000
Head of Household	$200,000
Qualifying Widower	$250,000

However, there is an exception for taxpayers who are residents of a treaty country for tax purposes. In this case, the resident could be considered a non-resident alien (NRA) for the purpose of NIIT, and thus not pay the 3.8% NIIT.

Additionally, spouses of U.S. citizens who make an election to be treated as U.S. residents for tax purposes are not subject to the NIIT on their income.

NIIT is certainly an issue for cryptocurrency investors, and can be a real reason to monitor the amount of gains in a year. Or living in Puerto Rico or expatriating are always options to get out from under

US tax laws.

3. DAOs AND MUTUAL FUNDS

The idea of decentralized autonomous organizations (DAOs) was eloquently defined in the Ethereum white paper that spawned the launching of new types of tokenized investment funds. The first was of course "The DAO," infamous for the hack of their smart contracts that led to the hard fork of Ether and Ethereum Classic. One thing that many people do not realize when investing in DAOs is that, under US law, if the company issuing is formed abroad, these fall under the punitive tax treatment for foreign mutual funds.

Like many areas in taxation, non-U.S. mutual funds were once a loophole that unscrupulous advisors used to help their wealthy clients avoid paying taxes. Because of these tough rules regarding passive foreign investment companies, or PFICs, income was passed to prevent there being any way to grow tax-free income in these accounts.

This can apply to a number of token investments, such as decentralized autonomous organizations (DAOs), as described in the original Ethereum white paper. These are investment funds that allow buyers to pool assets and vote on the investment of the proceeds into other assets. By definition, a PFIC is any company based outside the United States where more than 75% of the income comes from passive sources or more than 50% of the assets are held for the production of passive income. Thus a tokenized real estate investment or tokenized loan portfolio held outside the United States would also be a PFIC.

Foreign Mutual Funds

Sometimes in tax law you run across an area where a few greedy people ruined it for everyone else. One of those areas is foreign mutual funds. Investments in Passive Foreign Investment Companies (PFICs) used to be tax advantageous in that they only were taxed on the distributions. To close this loophole, new laws were formed with Section 1291 as introduced in the Tax Reform Act of 1986, and Form 8621 came into play. There are several elections on this complex form; I will only touch on them here. The most basic, and important item of note, is that 8621 is required to be filed *every* year you own this fund, unless you fall under the de minimus rule, which I will cover below.

The Qualified Electing Fund (QEF) election allows shareholders to have their pro-rata share of the earnings taxed in the current year, then not taxed on distribution. This cures the problem of deferral, preventing the penalty tax. The only problem is that non-U.S. mutual funds rarely issue statements with a breakdown of the earnings that would allow for a QEF election. Few tokenized venture offerings have determined how they will address this issue for investors.

An easier way to get around the penalties for marketable funds is with the Mark to Market (M2M) election. Using this method, the appreciation of the fund each year is added to income and taxed at ordinary rates. If there is a loss, it can be deducted up to the amounts of gains previously included in income. The price to prepare the returns still can be a costly part of compliance, as these are not simple forms to prepare, but at least the negative tax implications are minimized.

The M2M election must be made on a timely filed income tax return, another reason to be sure to stay up-to-date with filing. The negative tax implications of excess gains subject to the Section 1291 rules will still apply to years before the election was made, however it will stop penalty taxes from accruing for the future.

A Little Background

The complex rules surrounding PFIC income were passed as part of the Tax Reform Act of 1986, and as such have been around a lot longer than most people think. Prior to this, anyone could hold funds in foreign mutual funds and only pay tax on the dividends and capital gains. This meant that if you picked a fund that didn't pay out dividends and gains, your money could grow tax free until you took a distribution.

As is typical in the tax world, this was promoted by hucksters selling it to high-income taxpayers, and the government caught on. Much like how inversions were the hot topic recently, this was the political tax issue of the mid 1980s, and Congress enacted four different pieces of legislation to try and curb this prior to the 1986 tax reform.

This legislation not only sought to curb the tax benefits of this, but also tried to dissuade people from making these investments at all. As such, Congress instituted a strict method of taxation that, in essence, created a penalty tax. This certainly met the government's needs, but it has been a very harsh regime for many expats or unwitting U.S. citizens, and I have seen some extremely high tax bills resulting from PFIC income.

De Minimus Rule

Luckily, many taxpayers do not have to file the additional reporting requirements for their PFIC income. If the total amount of foreign mutual funds held in all accounts is $25,000 or less at the end of the year, then Form 8621 does not need to be filed. If both spouses are joint owners of the account and you file using the Married Filing Joint status, the amount increases to $50,000.

Pension Accounts

PFIC income that is held in pension accounts does not need to be reported on Form 8621 until distribution, simplifying the process for taxpayers with foreign retirement accounts. PFIC funds held in any US tax-free account, such as an IRA or 529 plan, do not ever need to be reported by the beneficial owner on Form 8621.

Qualified Electing Fund

Qualified Electing Fund (QEF) treatment is one of the most beneficial ways to treat PFIC income. Recognized income is limited to earnings and profits, and these can be treated as ordinary income from items such as interest or dividends, and long-term capital gains. Additionally, the ordinary income can be offset by capital losses before reporting. Win-win.

So why doesn't every shareholder in a PFIC elect QEF treatment? Unfortunately, there is a lot of reporting information that is required for making this election, and most foreign investment companies simply do not provide the documentation needed to make a QEF election.

Mark to Market

The next best treatment for PFIC income is electing Mark to Market (M2M) treatment. This can only be done for securities traded on some board or exchange, so it mainly applies to PFIC income from mutual funds rather than hedge funds or other alternate investments.

By claiming the M2M treatment, you only need to know three numbers—the value of shares at the start of the year, the value of shares at the end of the year, and value of any shares bought or sold during the year. This is much simpler than most tax practitioners make it out to be. Essentially, you net the end of year balance with the beginning of year balance and the gains are taxed every year as ordinary income. Then, when the mutual fund is sold, any gain or loss over the M2M position is reported at that time.

For most of my international clients, this is the beneficial treatment that leads to zero taxation. This is because, when taking the Foreign Earned Income Exclusion, typically all earned income will be wiped out, then unearned income such as this can be reported each year without paying tax, unless it exceeds the standard deduction amount. Thus having small amounts of the gain of the fund reported each year is far more beneficial for most than saving it up to report in one fell swoop when selling the mutual fund.

You cannot make an M2M election on an amended return—this must be done on a timely filed return. Excess gains are taxed in every year of the holding period on the individual's return. If there are gains beyond that when sold, these are also taxed.

Section 1291

For PFIC accounts where you do not make an election, they will be treated under the default rules of Section 1291, which essentially creates a penalty tax. Basically, the gain in the year of sale is considered to have been earned ratably over each year the fund was held, calculating penalties and interest on the gains in each year. This can add up to being a substantial tax amount!

Controlled Foreign Corporations

Companies cannot be treated as both Controlled Foreign Corporations (CFCs) and PFICs. Thus, if there is over 50% U.S. ownership, and at least one owner owns over 10% of the company, there may be an exception for this. However, then any owner holding 10% or more of the company will need to file the informational return for U.S.-held foreign corporations, Form 5471.

Being considered a Controlled Foreign Corporation is not necessarily a better tax treatment for U.S. owners now that the repatriation rules have come into effect with the Tax Cuts and Jobs Act. Additionally, it is still debatable if token holders would qualify for the percentage of ownership requirements for corporate ownership, as they do not hold equity.

Dividends

Dividends from foreign mutual funds are never considered qualified dividends, and given the lower long-term capital gains tax rate, this is not beneficial. This is true even in countries with tax treaties where otherwise a stock dividend would be treated under the qualified dividends rules. This is because it would be nearly impossible to prove that the underlying securities owned in the fund would meet the holding and treaty country requirements. Yet another reason why it is more tax advantageous to own individual securities than mutual funds.

Capital Losses

Capital losses from the sale of PFIC shares cannot be deducted on your tax return per Treasury Regulation 1.1291-6(b)(3). So it really is a double-edged sword that you can end up paying tax as one asset goes up, but you can't offset this by other PFIC investments losing money. Logical? Fair? No. But tax law is neither logical nor fair—that is why careful tax planning is so important.

4. FOREIGN EARNED INCOME EXCLUSION

If you're not already independently wealthy from your crypto holdings, one of the biggest advantages of moving outside the United States is getting to claim the Foreign Earned Income Exclusion (FEIE). This is how tax-free countries such as the United Arab Emirates have become hot for expat communities, attracting employees by offering such appealing benefits as six-figure tax-free salaries.

We should come right out and clarify that U.S. government employees such as military or diplomats are not eligible for the FEIE. Government contractors are often eligible, however, with certain restrictions. One point about government contractors to check is that they will always remain a resident of the state from where they moved away. This means government contracts may still have a hefty state tax liability, even if the Federal tax is fully waived.

Always Check Tax Credit First

If it is your first year of filing as an expat, you should always check if your tax is offset by the foreign tax credit before you commit yourself to filing the Foreign Earned Income Exclusion. Once you have started to file using Form 2555, if you fail to file this form in any other year where you have foreign earned income, you have revoked this right for the following five years.

FEIE Basics

Income for Foreign Earned Income Exclusion purposes includes your earned income and items such as housing credit. It does not, however, include employer contributions to pension plans.

There are two separate ways to qualify for the Foreign Earned Income Exclusion. One is the Physical Presence Test. That is the "330 days out of the year" method. The second is the Bona Fide Residence Test, which leaves it on you to show your true tax home is within a foreign country. When filing using Bona Fide, there are no time restrictions with being in the United States. We will go into this in more detail soon.

Earned Income Only

A deduction called the Foreign Earned Income Exclusion that only applies to earned income—who would've imagined that? Sometimes the IRS surprises us with their logical methodology just when we thought nothing related to tax could be based on logic. However, there are a few details to watch out for.

If income is earned on business trips to the United States, this income must be allocated in Form 2555 and reduces the available exclusion. This income can then be allocated onto a second foreign tax credit form, under the Resourced category, which I will discuss in the next chapter. To count your U.S. business travel dates, only count days you actually spent working, not travel days or personal days such as weekends.

This calculation gets far more complicated for pilots, flight attendants, and maritime workers. Days spent over international waters are considered U.S. travel dates, so intercontinental flights and open ocean voyages mean days when income earned cannot be excluded. Don't think you can get away with this either. There is a whole division in the IRS that audits these particular professions, and they will ask for flight plans or ship manifests to prove your locations. If you really don't go over international waters, be sure to keep up your documentation, as sooner or later you will get audited.

When filing Form 2555 to exclude self-employment income, it can also be a bit more complex than normal filings. The gross income from Schedule C is reported on line 20b and then the expenses are reported on line 44, reducing the amount of exclusion available. This seems to be a rather unfair way to calculate income and for those who have successful self-employment businesses, it is often advantageous to form a partnership or corporation in your home country. This way you may be able to take advantage of the full Foreign Earned Income Exclusion for your net income.

Risks of Revocation

Before I get into more of the technical items related to filing the Foreign Earned Income Exclusion, I want to bring up the inherent risk with filing this form. Once you have filed Form 5471 you must continue to file as long as you have foreign source income. If you do not file Form 5471 in a succeeding year, you will lose the right to file this form for the next five years. Yes, *five years*. That is a long time. Long enough that you don't know what will happen.

For example, if a revocation is made in 2015, you will not be able to file Form 2555 again until 2021! I have seen many times where clients elect to revoke this, then the next year, move to a tax-free country and regret their decision immensely.

If it is your first year filing U.S. taxes with foreign income, it is important to check if the Foreign Tax Credit will alleviate all tax due before filing the Foreign Earned Income Exclusion. Filing with just the Foreign Tax Credit in the first year of filing will give you dual benefits of keeping your options open for the future, and accumulating a foreign tax credit carryover. This is one of my biggest pet peeves when I get new clients transferring in from other tax preparers, or self-prepared returns. So many times people just file using Form 2555 without checking if there may be a better option, and this limits possibilities for the taxpayer in future years.

In practice, it has been possible to amend prior year returns to file Form 2555 when the election was accidentally revoked. I would not rely on this, however, as technically this election needs to be made on a timely filed return, and this could be disallowed. It does seem to pass through the service centers for now, though, and there is some documentation internally within the IRS's audit division of Large Business and International that allows for this. With the complexity of filing expat returns, the IRS has not quite caught up to uniformly enforcing all regulations, so many items are often allowed at the discretion of the reviewing agent. All amended returns are manually reviewed and undergo an internal audit procedure. This is especially true in the departments of the IRS that handle international tax returns.

It is important to note that if you move back to the United States, and thus cease filing Form 2555, then move overseas again in a later year, you will be allowed to file the exclusion again at this time. Not filing because of time spent in the United States does not constitute a revocation of the right to exclude foreign income as is clearly stated in the legislation related to this issue. However, if you continue to live in a foreign country and are unemployed, it is recommended to file Form 2555 with a nominal $1 of income added to preserve the filing pattern and not trigger an accidental revocation.

Physical Presence Test

This is the general test under which most people qualify. To meet the Physical Presence Test, you must have been physically outside the United States for 330 days out of any 365-day period. This is a little trickier to understand than it sounds, though.

The first item to understand is "outside the United States." This means days where you had zero presence in the United States or crossed international waters. Thus if you flew from Australia to Japan, technically this would count as a U.S. travel day. Airline pilots and flight attendants are commonly audited for this. The first thing that the IRS will ask about is records of the flight plans. More about this later.

The other half of this test is the 330-day period. Think of the year as a round circle with a 365-day period that can start on any day of the year and end exactly one year later. You can adjust this to cover any portion of the calendar year—even ending January 1 or starting December 31.

The key, though, is that the exclusion is only given for the period in the year that is included. If less than the full calendar year is a qualifying period, then the exclusion is prorated to only give the amount for the dates listed. This can limit the amount of exclusion allowed, which can have beneficial or painful consequences, depending on each individual's circumstances.

One time the Foreign Earned Income Exclusion can be really helpful is in the year of moving overseas. If you move to a country halfway through the tax year and don't take any trips back to the United States, then you can take an exclusion for a period of up to 35 days longer than the time you were in the United States. This is because the 365-day period can actually start up to 35 days before when you resided in the foreign country, and the period prior to the move is considered U.S. presence days. This can provide roughly $9,500 in additional exclusion. Pretty clever, right?

Keep in mind you cannot actually file your tax return until you have qualified for the Physical Presence Test with the dates filed. For example, if you moved overseas on June 1, 2017, and had no visits to the United States, your qualifying period could be April 28, 2017 through April 27, 2018. The earliest day you could file your 2017 tax return would be April 27, 2018. Luckily, U.S. residents living abroad are given an automatic extension until June 15 to file their tax returns, so you would not need to file an extension. But if you owed tax you would still want to pay by April 15 so as not to accrue any penalties. And often the easiest way to submit payment is with filing a Form 4868 extension, so this is not uncommon in this situation, although unnecessary.

This is one reason the Physical Presence Test is preferable over the Bona Fide Residence Test, which I will explain next. The other reason is that less personal information is required to qualify for the Physical Presence Test. And providing the least amount of information required to the IRS not only protects your privacy, but also gives them less reason to disallow the exclusion.

Bona Fide Residence Test

The Bona Fide Residence Test, because it is listed first on Form 2555, is often filled out more commonly than it should be. It is a nosy section that asks for a lot of personal information about who you live with, what your visa status is, and your ties to the United States. This is to try and determine your tax home so that the IRS can determine if you really are a "bona fide resident" of the country where you are living.

For some people, this is a non-issue and bona fide residence is clear. For example, if you have citizenship in the country of residence, own a house there, and are raising your children there, it is pretty clear. But if you still have numerous ties to the United States, spend significant time visiting family in the States, and stay in a house you own when you come back, then it points the other direction.

Certain people can never be considered bona fide residents of another country, such as civilian contractors working in support of military operations overseas. Not only are civilian contractors not bona fide residents, they are considered full-year residents of the last U.S. state where they resided. Thus they often have high state tax liabilities, even if owing no federal tax. California is especially rough in that they do not allow for any foreign earned income exclusion so all income earned overseas is fully taxable in California.

Who, then, you might ask, is this status good for? Well, the big benefit of qualifying for the Foreign Earned Income Exclusion using the Bona Fide Residence Test is that it allows for trips to the United States that total longer than 35 days. This can be very beneficial for those who travel frequently for business, as all those travel dates through the United States or over international waters add up fast. Also, some people have long holiday periods, such as school teachers, and they like to spend their two months off visiting family members stateside.

There is no waiting period for qualifying under the Bona Fide Residence Test; this can be claimed from the first year moving abroad. Before qualifying, though, you must have lived overseas for at least a full calendar year, meaning that your return will need to be on extension until at least January 1 of the following year in order to claim a full year. This may be confusing, so let me give an example. Say you move overseas on June 1, 2017. For filing your 2017 taxes, you would have a due date of June 15, 2018, but you could not file by then as you would have needed to live the full year of 2018 in your residence country to qualify for the Bona Fide Residence Test.

Thus you would need to file a special extension on Form 2350 to request the time to qualify for the Bona Fide Residence Test in addition to filing the standard extension on Form 4868.

International Waters

Any days that you fly over international waters or spend in the United States on business, you will need to pay U.S. tax on, regardless of where in the world you are living. This is because days spent over international waters or in transit to the United States are considered days spent in the United States that must be counted on the travel dates under either test

This can prove difficult for certain ship captains who may be residing in far off ports, but spending the bulk of their time transversing international waters. This is also a frequently audited issue for airline pilots and flight attendants. If you have one of these jobs, you can still spend time in the United States per the physical presence or bona fide residence rules without incurring additional tax—as long as you don't work in the United States or during cross-ocean flights.

Housing Exclusion

To increase your Foreign Earned Income Exclusion, you can add in the amount paid for housing, regardless of reimbursement. But it is important to note that reimbursement amounts are also considered income. Because this reimbursement is taxable, you have the option of taking the reimbursement amount or the total actual housing expenses paid, whichever is higher.

To figure the housing exclusion, you may deduct rent and utilities in addition, but not mortgage interest as that is deductible as an itemized deduction. There are limitations to the total amount that is deductible, then an additional amount is removed for what the IRS considers housing expenses would have been in the United States. The remaining portion is considered the housing exclusion and is added to the Foreign Earned Income and Housing Exclusion total that goes on line 21 of the 1040.

5. FOREIGN TAX CREDIT

The next great tax deduction that all crypto expats should know about is the foreign tax credit. Additionally, the credit can be claimed by those living in the United States with foreign income, but with additional limitations—especially with the new foreign corporation tax rules that came on board in 2017. In the spirit of preventing double taxation, this law allows you to take a credit of taxes you pay in other countries against your foreign income on your U.S. return. But be warned—there are many ways this is limited, as is normally the case with anything double-taxation related.

The foreign-earned income exclusion can be taken on its own or combined with the Foreign

Earned Income Exclusion to take a credit on any income that exceeds the exclusion amount. Keep in mind, though, that you cannot take both the foreign tax credit and the Foreign Earned Income Exclusion on the same income. Amounts must be allocated between them.

When filing the foreign tax credit, you will need to break up your income both by country and by type of income. Each various category of income type will be separated on a new copy of Form 1116. The income then is separated out on the 1116 by country. Income and taxes from multiple countries or varying types of income should never be combined together. There is one counter-intuitive exception to this country classification—if you receive income from an investment account usually the country it will be reported under will be "RIC," standing for "Registered Investment Company."

Check the Credit First

Before filing your first year of U.S. taxes living outside the United States, you should always check if the foreign tax credit will alleviate your tax liability before filing the Foreign Earned Income Exclusion. I just can't say this enough. This is one of the most common errors I see from individuals and tax professionals alike and it breaks my heart.

Once filing with the Foreign Earned Income

Exclusion, you have to keep filing that way or you revoke the use of it for five years. Filing with the foreign tax credit, your options are open for future years. Plus there are many other credits and tax advantages that are limited by the Foreign Earned Income Exclusion and can be fully taken alongside the credit.

The other big advantage of using the foreign tax credit from day one is that it creates a foreign tax credit carryover in most instances. This can add up over time to being very beneficial if you have a big year with a lot of tax hits.

This being said, you should only use the foreign tax credit if the results are the same or it is a minimal change. If the Foreign Earned Income Exclusion will give you bigger savings, then it is absolutely better to file that way from day one, as any sort of significant tax savings is always worth taking now, as the future is still uncertain.

Keep in mind this is also not always a black-and-white choice. There are many instances where you could exclude most of your income and still claim a foreign tax credit for passive income, employer pension contributions, U.S. business income, or other types of income that are not excludable. The point I wanted to make certain though is that the Foreign Earned Income Exclusion should not be your "go-to" choice without exploring all options.

General Category

The foreign tax credit requires that you break your income up into certain categories and report this separately, allocating the tax to each category. The first area to mention has to be the general category, as this is the earned income that most taxpayers have for at least a portion of their earnings.

General category includes income earned outside of the United States by personal work such as wages or self-employment. If you receive employer benefits such as housing or transportation allowances, a bonus, or severance pay, this is all considered general category income. This area also includes employer contributions to pension plans made on your behalf, in countries where this money is included in income, or you have elected to include this in income.

Income not included is from such sources as unemployment, dividends—even from a company you own—pension distributions, or income earned from a foreign country but while on U.S. business travel.

Even if filing using the Foreign Earned Income Exclusion, you can often also file a foreign tax credit for the general category to include income paid by your employer to your pension plan that cannot be excluded. This allows for a credit and building up a tax credit carryover, just as when excluding the bulk of your income.

Resourced Category

There is a much-misunderstood category of the foreign tax credit listed as "Certain Income Resourced by Treaty." This is where income earned on U.S. business travel goes, as this income was incorrectly taxed in your residence country. You can allocate based on a percentage of days.

Generally if filing the Foreign Earned Income Exclusion, I will use the software to make this allocation but if not filing the Foreign Earned Income Exclusion, I will divide total income by 240 days, then multiply by the number of days on U.S. business travel. Remember that transit days and weekends do not count—only actual work days that are spent on business in the United States are treated as business travel days during which that income was earned.

Some of the more complicated occupations for calculating this are airline pilots and flight attendants. If you work in one of these occupations, you will need to count all days where you cross over international waters on a flight plan as U.S. business dates. Upon IRS examination, one of the first things the agent will ask for is a list of your flight plans.

They will recalculate your income accordingly. If you do not do this yourself then you can wind up owing, as they likely will not give you as favorable of a tax allocation as if you filed correctly from the beginning.

Resourced category for U.S. business travel is often filed when using the Foreign Earned Income Exclusion in order to allocate taxes for the U.S. portion of income. This can both help in the year of filing and create a carryover for future years. Resourced category can only be taken in countries with a treaty that allows for U.S. business income to be taxed by the particular country, however, meaning this cannot be taken by just any U.S. taxpayer worldwide.

Passive Category

Passive category is the part of the foreign tax credit that is also commonly used by U.S. residents. Passive income commonly includes investments such as interest, dividends, and capital gains from stock sales. Also, most business income and real estate income will fall under the passive category. Most income from government sources such as unemployment, Social Security, and government pensions are also considered passive in nature.

One area where passive category foreign tax credit gets complex is that the income used for calculating this can only be income that is considered taxable in the country you are reporting tax from. This may sound obvious, but often isn't so clear in practice. Many countries have tax advantaged income where the income is excluded from taxation if under a certain threshold. This income should not be listed on Form 1116.

Important Adjustments

Certain items used to calculate income must be adjusted out of the foreign tax credit. If you are granted an adjustment to income for other tax items that are directly related to the income included on Form 1116, you must adjust out from the income used to calculate the foreign tax credit on these items. Common examples are moving expenses and the half of self-employment tax that is used as an adjustment to income.

It is also very important to make sure that the same income used for the Foreign Earned Income Exclusion is not included as income for the foreign tax credit. This "double dipping" is never allowed.

Calculating Foreign Tax Paid

I've covered the income side pretty extensively, but haven't really touched on the tax side of the equation. Not all foreign taxes are the same. The taxes that are deductible on the foreign tax credit are only income taxes. Many countries also impose social taxes and wealth taxes that are not eligible to be included on the foreign tax credit. Wealth taxes can usually still be included as an itemized deduction, but social taxes generally cannot be deducted at all.

In some countries this line can be rather blurred. If all the taxes are lumped together without any way to break them apart as line items, then the whole amount is typically includable on the foreign tax credit. Saudi Arabia is a good example of this with their mandatory 10% GOSI tax that at first doesn't seem to be includable, but I have always been told it counts as a tax to include on 1116. Still it is one of those areas where I wouldn't be surprised if someday that changes and new guidance comes out to the contrary. This is the way of the tax world, and especially for foreign and cryptocurrency taxes, as the information on how to file correctly is not as readily available as in other areas of tax practice.

6. Tax-Free Crypto Retirement Savings

Retirement plans formed in the United States can also be one of the best ways of investing in cryptocurrencies. If structured properly, self-directed IRA or 401(k) accounts can allow for tax-free growth of tokenized investments. In a self-directed 401k, it is possible to put away upwards of $50k per year of pre-tax money, then have the earnings grow tax free until distribution. Holding tokens within retirement accounts not only does defer or eliminates taxes, but it also eliminates the need for tedious record keeping of cryptocurrency trades.

Roth IRAs

Many people espouse the benefits of Roth IRAs, saying they are the best because earnings can be withdrawn tax free. And this certainly makes this one of the better tax saving accounts, especially for crypto investors. You contribute the money with after-tax money, meaning it doesn't reduce your taxes directly. But the money when you withdraw it is tax free, so if you plan to keep the funds growing for a long time, this will benefit you greatly. Also, these amounts may still qualify you for a saver's credit of 10–50% of your contribution amount if you meet the very low income restrictions to qualify.

There are income limitations on the top side as well regarding who can contribute to the Roth IRA, with the limits for single taxpayers being phased out between $116,000 and $131,000. In general, taxpayers in this bracket or above are not well served by contributing to a Roth IRA. More often they would benefit more from taking a deduction against their taxable income by contributing to a traditional IRA account.

An additional benefit to a Roth IRA is that the contributions, but not earnings, can be taken out at any time without penalty. So it gives more flexibility if an emergency comes up and the funds are needed.

Keep in mind that if the earnings are withdrawn early, they are subject both to income tax and the 10% additional penalty tax, so it is not wise to fully cash out a Roth IRA.

Plans Outside the United States

Saving for retirement is encouraged worldwide, but few other countries have plans that are considered qualified—meaning treated the same as a 401(k) or IRA would be within the United States. Therefore one must be very careful because an account may be tax advantaged in your home country but end up costing you tax-wise on your U.S. return. This info may not apply to many of the crypto crowd, but is still worth covering, just in case.

Many times taxpayers think that because an investment is not taxable in their home country it will also not be taxable in the United States. But rarely is this the case. More often than not, the United States will tax you on your investment and retirement accounts. What comes as the biggest surprise, though, for many taxpayers is that pension contributions made to their retirement account by their employers are considered income and taxable immediately.

Switzerland and Australia come to mind on this front. In those countries, it is required that an employer contribute to the pension plans of employees, yet this is not considered taxable income —or even very clearly told to the employee. Thus it is often a confusing and difficult process to get the paperwork showing the contributions made by the employer, which is needed to report the accurate amount of gross income for the year.

Qualified Plans

Certain countries have what are known as "Qualified" retirement plans, meaning the employer contributions are not required to be included in taxable income for U.S. persons. The four countries that have qualified plans are:

United Kingdom

Netherlands

Germany

Belgium

Even though it is not required, you may still want to include your contributions in income if below the FEIE, as this will create a basis for when you take distributions to reduce your taxable income. To benefit from this you need to track your annual contributions—forever. From experience, though, most taxpayers do not track things that well— especially when there is only one entry per year—

thus this only benefits very organized people.

When taking distributions, it is common to apply a percentage that approximates the taxable contribution basis. For most taxpayers, this is sufficient. But if you think you can track this forever and want the extra savings come retirement, it certainly wouldn't hurt to start a spreadsheet and track this amount each year.

Self-Directed Foreign Pensions

When taxpayers have self-directed foreign pensions, they often get into a tremendous amount of U.S. tax filing complexity. I see this commonly in Australia and New Zealand, where Superannuation and Kiwi Saver plans, respectively, can be organized into an account where the taxpayer has control over the investments, and even can own real estate and businesses in them.

This generally means that foreign trust returns must be filed, as well as sometimes generating returns for reporting foreign corporations or disregarded entities, and sometimes generating Passive Foreign Investment Company (PFIC) reporting requirements as well. As this can mean thousands of dollars in U.S. tax preparation fees a year, this is only an intelligent investment choice for taxpayers with significant retirement assets.

Canadian RRSPs and RRIFs

Canadian retirement accounts such as RRSP and RRIF funds previously needed to be reported annually in the United States on Form 8891, however, revenue procedure 2014-55 abolished the need to file this form. Now U.S. citizens and residents who own RRSP and RRIF forms automatically qualify for tax deferral similar to how a 401k or IRA account is treated in the United States.

IRA Accounts

Self-directed IRA accounts can be an excellent way to hold token investments. These accounts allow for deferred or entirely tax-free treatment, and also eliminate many of the hassles of record keeping and reporting of trades.

Individual Retirement Arrangements, known generally as "IRAs," are U.S. retirement accounts that have special tax treatment. These accounts allow you to contribute up to the yearly maximum of $5,500 for 2015, as long as you are within the income limitations, and you have earned income in at least the amount of the contribution. If you exclude all your earned income with the Foreign Earned Income Exclusion, you may not qualify for making a contribution to an IRA account. Nonetheless, you often can allow enough income to flow through with using the Physical Presence Test on Form 2555 to allow income for claiming an IRA deduction.

Depending on where you keep your IRA account, you will have various choices for investments. Some IRA trustees only allow you to invest in a few mutual funds they offer. Others, such as the ones at online brokerages, allow you to invest in any stock market investment. You may also have a "self-directed IRA" with certain trustees where you can invest in real estate or other investments. No matter who has your account, you are not allowed to invest in collectibles, such as art, antiques, or coins.

It is important to minimize the fees in your IRA account. High fees can have a drastic effect on the amount of money in your account down the line. The average fee for mutual funds in the United States is 3.14%! This can greatly reduce your retirement funds.

> If you invest $100,000 at age 35 and get a 7% annualized return, at age 65 you will have $324,340 in your account if you are paying 3% in fees.
>
> But if you are paying only 1% in fees at age 65 your account will have $574,349.
>
> **That difference is nearly double the amount, for only two percentage points of fees!**

Generally, the lowest fees are with online brokerage accounts, many of which only charge you for trades and don't assess any annual fees. The highest fees are generally with hedge funds or self-directed IRAs. In the right circumstances, with the best advice and luck, these accounts can pay off and be worth the fees. Especially with the potential gains of cryptocurrency and ICO investments, self-directed retirement accounts can be a worthwhile structure to establish for holding these investments.

Many expat taxpayers mistakenly think they are not qualified to contribute to IRA accounts in the United States, but this is not the case. The qualifications for contributing to IRA accounts and their tax deductibility is the same to U.S. citizens the world over with one important difference—income excluded as the Foreign Earned Income Exclusion is not eligible to be used as income toward qualifying for an IRA account. This can be easily remedied if using the Physical Presence Test for qualifying on Form 2555 by adjusting the dates in order to allow income to flow through. However, you must carefully watch your U.S. travel dates when doing this, as well as following special procedures to not get into trouble with the Affordable Care Act. If you are in this situation, I would not recommend trying this on your own. Definitely seek out experienced help to make these adjustments.

7. BEACHSIDE RETIREMENT INCOME

Retiring abroad is the dream of the crypto beach movement. This dream is alluring to many, especially when moving somewhere less expensive that can lead to allowing your investment dollars to stretch for longer. While many in the crypto investment world may only have tokenized investments, others have a combination of crypto and fiat-based investments. If leaving a job, you always need to be careful about employers trying to cash out your retirement plans, as this often generates a large tax burden by both raising the tax rate and triggering a 10% penalty tax.

Calculating U.S. tax on retirement income is simple if it is solely U.S. based, but if you have paid into retirement plans in multiple countries this can create a complex tax situation. This can certainly come into play for those who follow the tactics in the previous chapter to build up cryptocurrency investments in tax-advantaged accounts.

Social Security Income

While there are many areas of tax law that have advantages for U.S. residents living abroad, Social Security income is certainly not one of them. U.S. Social Security can be taxed by the United States, as well as being additionally taxed by foreign countries. Within the United States, the amount of tax levied on Social Security is on an income-based scale that adds somewhere between zero and 85% of the Social Security income in to the taxable mix.

There are parts of various tax treaties that make it sound like this shouldn't be the case, but with a few notable exceptions, the treaties aren't written in such a way where they give significant benefit to U.S. citizens.

A few countries have the significant benefit where resident U.S. citizens will not pay any U.S. tax on U.S. Social Security received. This also goes the other direction, however, so if you receive Social Security from the country where you are a resident, it is fully taxable under U.S. law, even if it is tax free in the country where you receive it.

For example, if you are a resident of Germany and receive both Social Security and the Social Code, the German equivalent, you would pay U.S. tax on the Social Code, but zero U.S. tax on Social Security.

Countries Where U.S. Citizens are Exempt from Tax on Social Security if residents:
Canada
Egypt
Germany
Ireland
Israel
Italy*
Romania
United Kingdom
*Must be an Italian Citizen.

In other countries there is no exemption from U.S. tax, but the local social security is not taxable in the United States under the treaty. (Austria)

Sifting through the Treaties

Treaties must be carefully read and interpreted in order to understand which income they are exempting. Do not assume that because a treaty is in place that it is in your favor. Switzerland, for example, taxes U.S. Social Security without giving any credit and, in addition, Swiss Social Security benefits are taxable on the U.S. tax return, creating a double-taxation burden that has no relief under the terms of the treaty.

French Social Security is not taxable on your U.S. return by treaty, contrasted with U.S. Social Security payments being non-taxable income when living in Israel and several other countries. When living in Italy, you must be an Italian citizen to be exempt from U.S. tax on your Social Security. Much of what sounds like tax relief in treaties will be overridden by the Savings Clause and then in some cases there are exceptions to the Savings Clause, overriding that as well. Only for full-year residents of a foreign country without U.S. citizenship or green cards do treaty positions apply in full.

Swiss residents who receive U.S. Social Security are subject to a substantial double tax burden. The U.S. taxes up to 85% of the Social Security benefits received, and Switzerland also taxes this at full rates without offering any credit. In the reverse situation when U.S. residents receive Swiss Social Security, Switzerland does not tax the payments—only the United States does. If Switzerland did tax the payments though, the United States would offer a credit based on the general provisions of paragraph 2, article 23 of the treaty.

Confusing, right? These treaties are quite a mess!

Residents of the United Kingdom are exempt on their U.S. taxes the amount of taxation that would be exempt under U.K. law. Thus 15% of U.K. state pensions (the equivalent of U.S. Social Security) are exempt, and 25% of private employer pensions in the United Kingdom are exempt. However, lump-sum payouts from a U.K. pension are fully taxable under U.S. law. On the other hand, U.S. Social Security is fully exempt from taxation to U.K. residents.

Pensions

Pension accounts that are rolled over into plans within the same plan category have no taxable consequence. Similar rules to U.S. qualified rollovers must be followed. (The rules for this are complex and beyond the scope of this book, but there are many resources available for this.) An example would be rolling funds over from one non-qualified foreign pension to another non-qualified foreign pension. On a side note, annuities have the same tax treatment as pensions.

Foreign Pension Distributions

When receiving income from foreign pension accounts, it is treated in much the same way as U.S. retirement accounts. In most countries, as the plans are not considered qualified, the contributions by both the employee and employer are considered after-tax contributions, meaning that only the earnings in the account are taxed on distribution, not the contributions themselves, also known as "basis" in tax-speak. This is treated similar to distributions from a traditional IRA when non-deductible contributions were made.

Sometimes it can be difficult to determine the correct amount of basis though, as records are often not kept for the entire lifespan of the pension. It is oftentimes obvious that some portion of the income should be determined to be non-taxable, but it can be impossible to get the exact amount. In practice, I have seen percentages of 30–60% applied as basis, depending on the age of the retiree and the types of investments that were allowed in the account, i.e., in countries like Australia, where the standard is very conservative investments, it may be reasonable to apply 60% as basis (meaning just 40% of the income is taxable), but in countries like Switzerland, where most pensions are invested in more aggressive portfolio mixes, then a 40% basis might be more reasonable.

8. UNIVERSAL TAX DEDUCTIONS

A Taxing Life

I'll share with you a dirty secret—we're taxed much higher as U.S. citizens than most people admit. From someone who has seen financials the world over, few countries are more highly taxed than us—most notably the United Kingdom. This especially becomes apparent when you add up all the different taxes that Americans pay: income tax, Social Security, Medicare, unemployment insurance, and state and local income taxes are just the start. Then, of course, we have sales tax, property tax, gasoline tax, alcohol tax—the list goes on and on. Most items you purchase in the United States have been taxed five times before you take them home.

I won't get in to where that money goes. That is another great frustration for most citizens—and a large driver of expatriations. The bottom line, though, is this usually feels like money down the drain, especially for crypto purists.

Itemized Deductions

I'll save you a lot of time here. Especially after the Tax Cuts and Jobs Act, very few taxpayers will qualify to itemize deductions. Unless you own a house with a mortgage under $750,000 but a high percentage rate or make a massive charitable contribution, you will most likely not have any benefit from itemizing deductions. Why? Under the new tax law you are given a standard deduction amount of $12,000 if you are single, or double that if married. In the past, you also received personal exemptions for dependents whether itemizing or not, but that is gone. Most people just don't pay more than that in the types of expenses that can be taken as a deduction.

Itemized Deductions (Schedule A)

We will use an example here of an expat "friend" who earns roughly $150,000 and takes the Foreign Earned Income Exclusion, bringing Adjusted Gross Income (AGI) down to around $50,000.

Medical and Dental Expenses

For this category, you will not see the first dollar of expenses until you have more expenses than the 7.5% AGI floor. Miles driven for medical purposes are also deductible, at a lowered rate now after the Tax Cuts and Jobs Act.

Our friend pays $220/mo in insurance and had a rough year where she was really sick with ten doctor visits of $50, prescriptions of $250 and a dentist visit that cost $800.

- Insurance: $2,640.00

- Doctor Visits: $500

- Prescriptions: $250

- Dentist: $800

- Medical Miles: 300 x 17¢/mi = $51

Total Medical Expenses: $4,241

AGI Floor: $150,000 x 7.5%(0.75) = $3,750

Medical Deduction: $4,241 - $3,750 = $491

Taxes You Paid:

This section is for state taxes and real estate taxes. The Tax Cuts and Jobs Act limited this to $10,000 max.

Our friend owns a house and pays property tax but does not pay any U.S. state tax.

- Real Property Taxes Paid: $2,016

Deductible Taxes: $2,016

Interest Deduction:

This is where mortgage interest comes into play. The recent law changes limited the amount of mortgage interest you can take to $750,000 of loan value, and only for a loan used to buy or renovate your home (home equity loans are no longer deductible).

Our friend pays a mortgage on her home with a loan less than $750,000:

- Mortgage Interest Paid: $8,603

Deductible Interest: $8,603

Gifts to Charity:

Charitable contributions are deductible, but only for contributions made to qualified U.S. charities. Thus most expat filers will not have charitable contributions for U.S.

tax purposes.

Our friend did not have any charitable contributions.

Casualty and Theft Losses:

The Tax Cuts and Jobs Act changed it where casualty losses can only be taken for federally declared disaster zones and thus will not apply for most expats.

Our friend did not have any casualty or theft losses.

Job Expenses and Misc. Deductions

The Tax Cuts and Jobs Act removed all miscellaneous deductions such as those for job expenses. Thus they will no longer be deductible.

Our friend was not allowed to take miscellaneous deductions as they are no longer deductible.

Adding up all the deductions for our friend, we come up with the following:

Total Itemized Deductions: $491 + $2016 + $8,016= $10,523

This amount is less than the standard deduction our friend receives of $12,000, meaning there is no benefit for her to itemize deductions this year.

Unless your itemized deductions are a good bit higher than the standard deduction it is not worthwhile to itemize. This is because itemizing increases the likelihood of audit, which is a hassle and an expense that exposure to should be minimized, when viable. Also, if you have U.S. source income where you receive a state tax refund, you will end up having to include this state tax refund as income the following year. This will increase your adjusted gross income, limiting credits and deductions the next year. Sometimes this is still worthwhile, but must be justified by a significant tax savings this year. You now get an idea of the types of things good accountants weigh out when preparing your return. It is not as simple as most people think.

There are a couple of instances where you will need to itemize deductions, regardless of if it benefits you, such as if you are married and filing separately from your spouse and your spouse itemizes deductions. But for the sake of simplicity, I will leave this just at the basics that have already been covered, as most crypto expats simply won't itemize.

Education and Child Credits

Credits are preferable to deductions in many ways. They give a bigger "bang for the buck" than deductions as they come off the bottom line. This means they directly offset the tax owed, dollar for dollar. Generally, when you hear Congress talking about a "stimulus package" of any sort, this will mean some kind of tax credit is coming. Whether the credits will be for businesses or individuals depends on the administration, as well as what goals they are trying to accomplish.

Education credits right now are rather valuable, as far as credits go. The American Opportunity Tax Credit has the advantage of being a refundable credit, meaning you can get a refund without having paid in any taxes! Many expat taxpayers do not know that some foreign institutions are considered eligible U.S. institutions for the education credits.

Education credits are limited to amounts you paid for actual education costs, generally limited to just tuition, fees, books, and so forth. This means you can't deduct your housing costs, even if you paid for on-campus housing. The maximum credit is $2,500, and up to $1,000 of that is refundable.

Some of the best credits in the tax code are related to children. The Child Tax Credit gives you up to $2,000 per child as a credit, of which $1,400 is potentially refundable, allowing for a refund even when tax has not been paid in. Additionally there is a $500 credit for non-child dependents.

This credit requires earned income and as such for many expat filers who use the Foreign Earned Income Exclusion is not applicable. We used to be able to work around this, but the PATH Act closed these loopholes. Now if you use the Foreign Earned Income Exclusion, you are barred from receiving the refundable Child Tax Credit.

The Earned Income Tax Credit (EITC) is another income-based tax credit for which many families with children in the United States qualify. To claim this credit, the children must live with you in the United States for at least half the year, and EITC is never allowed if using the Foreign Earned Income Exclusion. Thus this credit will almost never be seen on a crypto expat return.

Retirement Contributions

Retirement contributions are one of the few ways you can reduce your income after the end of the tax year. I have already covered retirement contributions in depth, but what is important to note here is that you can contribute to an IRA account until April 15 of the year following the close of the tax year, meaning

Dormant Corporation Under Rev. Proc. 92-70

- Less than $100,000 in assets
- Less than $5,000 in income
- Less than $5,000 in expenses
- No transactions related to the stock

if you file your taxes early, this can be a place to save.

This can be advantageous to some expat taxpayers who have exceeded the Foreign Earned Income Exclusion and can reduce their adjusted gross income below certain thresholds using a deductible IRA contribution in order to qualify for credits or deductions that would be otherwise lost.

Alternative Minimum Tax

After the Tax Cuts and Jobs Act very few taxpayers in general will have expenses that trigger the dreaded alternative minimum tax (AMT), so I will keep this section very short. However, as it is so commonly misunderstood, I felt that I should cover it here.

Simplified Method

The IRS has come out with a simplified method of calculating AMT that often comes up with a tax liability when using this method, when no AMT would be triggered otherwise. I would recommend not ever using this method. And if you do see AMT showing on a tax return, one of the first things I would look for is if the "simplified" box was checked on Form 6251.

Changing Filing Status

The trigger points for AMT are triggered by both gross income and filing status. Sometimes, if you qualify, you may change your filing status to Head of Household by adding a non-resident alien dependent, or even adding a non-resident alien spouse to file jointly by applying for an ITIN.

Capital Gains/Qualified Dividends

The preferential tax rates that apply to capital gains income and qualified dividends is sometimes enough to trigger AMT. A common occurrence is that capital losses will reduce tax, then AMT adds it back in. There is little that can be done in this very frustrating situation. These are valid reasons for AMT, as are high employee business expenses reported as part of the itemized deductions.

9. LAUNCHING AN INTERNATIONAL BUSINESS

There has been much talk in the media the past few years of U.S. corporations relocating abroad in order to save on taxes. Owning a business overseas can have some big tax advantages if structured properly, or can be very expensive if not planned with tax considerations in mind, especially after the Tax Cuts and Jobs Act. In this chapter I will discuss the basics of foreign companies including self-employment and partnerships, and in the next chapter I will go more in detail to discussing the U.S. corporations and the filing requirements.

Self-Employment

When most entrepreneurs start a company, they do so as a solo entrepreneur. If you do this, or take contract labor on, you are considered self-employed under the eyes of the U.S. government. This distinction is usually rather clear cut when living within the United States, as your employer will send you either Form 1099-MISC for self-employment or Form W-2 for wages at the end of the year, and then you report the income accordingly. But for business ventures or international income sources this determination can be more murky.

Cryptocurrency mining is the term used when you run a computer program that solves complex equations in the process of validating transactions on the network. Mining of cryptocurrencies is considered self-employment under U.S. tax law, so this can be a surprise to many casual miners who get coins as a result of running software on their computer. But for larger mining operations, this is more obvious as the computer resources and energy usage can be substantial.

Mining is only one method of receiving additional cryptocurrency tokens. Mining is used on proof-of-work (POW) systems that have been criticized for extensive resource usage. There are other proofing systems such as proof-of-stake (POS), where nodes made up of tokens verify transactions and are awarded new tokens based on how many tokens are held by each node. Other systems, such as proof-of-capacity, are based on renting storage space, which would seem to be providing resources and fall under the category of business income.

Staking is a little less clear when determining if it would be considered a business venture. I could see the stronger argument about staking tokens being that they are an investment. This is because there are few computer resources utilized and the main cost is typically in the purchase of the tokens used to stake the nodes. Thus it would seem the award of tokens could be a passive return on investment rather than self-employment earnings. But it could be argued the other direction that by setting up nodes and verifying transactions, active work is being performed, and as such would be considered business income.

Under U.S. tax law, if you are a U.S. citizen or resident and have self-employment income, you are obligated to contribute to Social Security and Medicare the same as if you lived in the United States. There are some exceptions for tax treaty countries, which I will get into later in this chapter, but first it's best to understand the difference between an employee and an independent contractor.

Independent Contractors

If you have determined you are really an independent contractor, you may next be wondering which tax forms you need to file. Schedule C is the form that is attached to your U.S. return to show your income and expenses from a business. First, some Schedule C basics:

Schedule C Tips
i. Always use the correct NAICS code to describe your business. NEVER use code 999999 as lack of classification raises risk for audit.
ii. Be sure to use your foreign address on Schedule C even if you use a U.S. address for business.
iii. Use the right accessory forms— Business use of Home, Auto Expenses and Depreciation all have special uses and if reported wrong can open you up for big liability.
iv. Separate out meals & entertainment expenses from travel. This can seem like a bit of a thin line, but meal expenses you are only allowed to deduct 50% of, so it is important these are properly separated.

Schedule C expenses are a bit less beneficial for expats than for U.S. residents, as expenses reported on Schedule C reduce your Foreign Earned Income Exclusion. When filling out Form 2555, full income from business must be included, then the expenses on Schedule C as well as half of your SE tax and other adjustments to income related to business are deducted on line 44.

This is a huge disadvantage of owning a sole proprietorship overseas, even in tax treaty countries, and is one reason I recommend owning a foreign corporation for many clients. The added complexity and cost of Form 5471 is well worthwhile if it saves huge money in Foreign Earned Income Exclusion and SE tax.

Tax Treaties Excluding SE Tax

Certain countries have tax treaties that if you pay into the social security system of that country, then you do not need to pay into the U.S. Social Security system.

> Tax Tip: This is a highly audited area. I would recommend if you are self-employed getting a letter from your local social security office in your country of residence proving you pay into this system. This way you will be covered if audited down the line.

If you have both wages and self-employment

income and live in a country that has a tax treaty, you are in luck—even if you don't pay in on your self-employment income, you do not need to pay the SE tax. Why is this the case? The reason behind tax treaties for social security taxes paid is not to help workers get out of paying twice. It is to keep you from contributing to more than one system in the same year and accumulating credits in multiple countries at the same time. And just when you thought the government had your best interests in mind for once.

If the IRS questions your deduction, you may need to obtain a certificate of coverage from the social security office in your country of residence. This is not required to claim the exclusion, and if you properly reference the treaty and the date this was signed into force, this information should not be necessary, but on occasion the IRS sends out an audit letter asking for it anyway.

With this overhanging threat in mind, it is a good idea to get this letter from the social security office before you move away from a country if you have claimed the SE tax treaty exclusion. The IRS will ask for a certified translated copy also, so if there is an option to get this document in English, I would suggest doing that to save yourself an extra step if it is ever requested. Once you provide the certificate once, you will not be requested to send it again, or that has been my experience at least.

Countries with Social Security Agreements	
Country	*Entry into Force*
Australia	October 1, 2002
Austria	November 1, 1991
Belgium	July 1, 1984
Canada	August 1, 1984
Chile	December 1, 2001
Czech Republic	January 1, 2009
Denmark	October 1, 2008
France	July 1, 1988
Finland	November 1, 1992
Germany	December 1, 1979
Greece	September 1, 1994
Ireland	September 1, 1993
Italy	November 1, 1978
Japan	October 1, 2005
Luxembourg	November 1, 1993
Norway	July 1, 1984
Netherlands	November 1, 1990
Poland	March 1, 2009
Portugal	August 1, 1989
Slovak Republic	May 1, 2014
South Korea	April 1, 2001
Spain	April 1, 1988
Sweden	January 1, 1987
Switzerland	November 1, 1980
United Kingdom	January 1, 1985

Joint Ventures

So, what if you own a business with your spouse? What if your spouse is a non-resident alien and owns a business—does this count towards ownership for you?

Splitting income and expenses in half is not always the most accurate way to do this, although this what is required. This is another reason why creating a corporation in these situations can be more beneficial.

Partnerships

Partnerships are fairly straightforward, but the income is reported a bit differently. It should not be placed on Schedule C, but net income should be listed directly on line 21. Depending on the ownership percentage, Form 8865 may need to be filed.

Limited Liability Structures

By default, any type of foreign company formation with a limited liability structure is considered a foreign corporation under U.S. law, regardless of what the entity type is called in another country. This can lead to much confusion among tax professionals, as in the United States a limited liability company (LLC) has default classification as a partnership or sole-proprietorship. Many foreign countries now offer LLCs for formation that are similar to the ones in the United States, yet under U.S. tax law, these foreign LLCs would be considered corporations.

You may elect to have this income treated in a different classification by filing Form 8832 to elect tax treatment of your entity. This is not usually recommended, however. In general, treatment under corporate regulations is more beneficial tax-wise than electing to be treated in a different way.

Disregarded Entities

I have seen an increasing trend in accountants recommending for clients to file the election to have their partnership or corporation treated as a disregarded entity. I would strongly recommend against doing this for several reasons, the main one being that by electing to be a disregarded entity you lose many of the tax benefits inherent in the foreign income structure. My guess is that this is advised in a misguided attempt to help clients simplify their taxes. But this is not the case, as with a disregarded entity you must still file Form 8858 each year, a form just as complex as Form 5471, and you must also file Schedule C to report the income directly on your return. This adds cost and complexity to a return without providing any benefit.

Whatever kind of company you own, do

remember that returns of expats are more highly audited, so are business returns, thus, you are running a dual risk of audit by filing with both of these elements in your return. It is therefore critical that you have substantiation for your deductions archived and that you fully understand and file according to the laws. These days ,with so many apps that are cloud based to help you organize and archive receipts, there is no excuse to not keep good records.

10. FOREIGN CORPORATIONS

If you are a blockchain entrepreneur raising money from an ICO worldwide, Form 5471 is your new best friend. Although one of the most complex tax forms to prepare, there are few areas you can legally save greater money on taxes than in properly structuring and filing for your foreign corporation. This is why corporations such as Google and General Electric have moved billions of dollars offshore in recent years.

This is especially the case after the Tax Cuts and Jobs Act, on top of the previous myriad tax treaties and vague regulations. There are many loopholes still to exploit, although loopholes are closed all the time. Foreign partnerships do not have much of the benefits of foreign corporations; I mainly see them used in countries like the United Kingdom where taxes often exceed the United States and corporate law is less friendly domestically.

There is a third option for foreign entities and that is to be filed to be treated as a foreign disregarded entity and then annually filing Form 8858. This is another complex and costly form to file every year, and gives none of the tax separation benefits available with the foreign corporation or foreign partnership, so I rarely recommend this.

Offshoring Controversy

There is much controversy right now as mega corporations shift their main operations overseas in order to legally—but semi-ethically—reduce taxes. I would never recommend this for U.S. companies, as anything done out of avoidance of taxes is bound to lead to trouble down the line. Big corporations like Microsoft and Pfizer can get away with this to squeeze out increased profits because they have the legal teams available to fight for them. Smaller companies, on the other hand, are more likely to be made examples of. Still, for entrepreneurial expats who live overseas, there are many ways to take advantage of these laws in fully legal and ethical ways.

Depending how structured, foreign corporations can earn income and keep it within the company as retained earnings, without paying out a dollar in tax. You read that right. The company can earn money and if it isn't paid out, it isn't subject to tax. There are rules about this, of course, and getting caught doing things the wrong way is very costly.

Foreign corporations can also be very beneficial tax-wise because the wages paid to a U.S. person who also lives overseas can be excluded with the Foreign Earned Income Exclusion. In addition, if living in a tax treaty country for qualified dividends (see chapter 2), all dividends received from a foreign corporation that you have owned the full year will be taxed at the long-term capital gains tax rates.

Benefits of an Offshore Corporation

In order to maximize the tax benefits of an offshore corporation is to generate retained earnings that are not paid out of the company as dividends or wages. This way you can keep the retained earnings growing on a tax-deferred basis inside the company indefinitely. But there are some exceptions to this, the main one being not to fall into having Subpart F income, which I will get into in a little bit.

They also can be very beneficial tax-wise because the wages paid to a U.S. person who also lives overseas can be excluded with the Foreign Earned Income Exclusion. In addition, if living in a tax treaty country for qualified dividends (see chapter xxx), all dividends received from a foreign corporation that will be taxed at the long-term capital gains tax rates. For this to be the case, though, you must own the property for the holding periods, generally though it is not an issue with dividends from foreign corporations not being qualified, unless issued in the year the company was acquired.

Popular Countries for Forming Corporations

Just as certain states within the United States are more friendly toward corporations, the same is true internationally. Certain countries go beyond being tax havens to having corporate laws that are friendly both for taxes and for protecting investors.

Topping the list of investment-friendly locales, the Cayman Islands has corporate law structured much like the investor-friendly state of Delaware. With a long history of protecting investor rights and privacy, this country reigns supreme both for those who want to legally structure their assets to manage

Foreign Entities Classified as Corporations for Federal Tax Purposes:	

American Samoa—Corporation	Kazakstan—Ashyk Aktsionerlik Kogham
Argentina—Sociedad Anonima	Republic of Korea—Chusik Hoesa
Australia—Public Limited Company	Latvia—Akciju Sabiedriba
Austria—Aktiengesellschaft	Liberia—Corporation
Barbados—Limited Company	Liechtenstein—Aktiengesellschaft
Belgium—Societe Anonyme	Lithuania—Akcine Bendroves
Belize—Public Limited Company	Luxembourg—Societe Anonyme
Bolivia—Sociedad Anonima	Malaysia—Berhad
Brazil—Sociedade Anonima	Malta—Public Limited Company
Bulgaria—Aktsionerno Druzhestvo	Mexico—Sociedad Anonima
Canada—Corporation and Company	Morocco—Societe Anonyme
Chile—Sociedad Anonima	Netherlands—Naamloze Vennootschap
People's Republic of China—Gufen Youxian	New Zealand—Limited Company
Gongsi	Nicaragua—Compania Anonima
Republic of China (Taiwan) —Ku-fen Yu-hsien	Nigeria—Public Limited Company
Kung-szu	Northern Mariana Islands—Corporation
Colombia—Sociedad Anonima	Norway—Allment Aksjeselskap
Costa Rica—Sociedad Anonima	Pakistan—Public Limited Company
Croatia—Dionicko Drustvo	Panama—Sociedad Anonima
Cyprus—Public Limited Company	Paraguay—Sociedad Anonima
Czech Republic—Akciova Spolecnost	Peru—Sociedad Anonima
Denmark—Aktieselskab	Philippines—Stock Corporation
Ecuador—Sociedad Anonima or Compania	Poland—Spolka Akcyjna
Anonima	Portugal—Sociedade Anonima
Egypt—Sharikat Al-Mossahamah	Puerto Rico—Corporation
El Salvador—Sociedad Anonima	Romania—Societe pe Actiuni
Estonia—Aktsiaselts	Russia—Otkrytoye Aktsionernoy
European Economic Area/European Union —	Obshchestvo
Societas Europaea	Saudi Arabia—Sharikat Al-Mossahamah
Finland—Julkinen Osakeyhtio/Publikt	Singapore—Public Limited Company
Aktiebolag	Slovak Republic—Akciova Spolocnost
France—Societe Anonyme	Slovenia—Delniska Druzba
Germany—Aktiengesellschaft	South Africa—Public Limited Company
Greece—Anonymos Etairia	Spain—Sociedad Anonima
Guam—Corporation	Surinam—Naamloze Vennootschap
Guatemala—Sociedad Anonima	Sweden—Publika Aktiebolag
Guyana—Public Limited Company	Switzerland— Aktiengesellschaft
Honduras—Sociedad Anonima	Thailand—Borisat Chamkad (Mahachon)
Hong Kong—Public Limited Company	Trinidad and Tobago—Limited Company
Hungary—Reszvenytarsasag	Tunisia—Societe Anonyme
Iceland—Hlutafelag	Turkey—Anonim Sirket
India—Public Limited Company	Ukraine—Aktsionerne Tovaristvo Vidkritogo
Indonesia—Perseroan Terbuka	Tipu
Ireland—Public Limited Company	United Kingdom—Public Limited Company
Israel—Public Limited Company	United States Virgin Islands—Corporation
Italy—Societa per Azioni	Uruguay—Sociedad Anonima
Jamaica—Public Limited Company	Venezuela—Sociedad Anonima or Compania
Japan—Kabushiki Kaisha	Anonima

taxes, and those who are illegally evading their obligations. This comes at a cost, however, as

Cayman corporations are perhaps more closely scrutinized by the IRS than those formed in other countries. Additionally, many island nations with favorable tax regimes have been black-listed by European countries, triggering punative taxes if living there.

Some have gone so far as to say that one should obtain a private letter ruling to support the legal standing, but I would say that is a bit extreme. However, as with any item that could be considered a tax strategy, a legitimate business purpose that is non-tax related should be at the core of this decision. For many business owners the possibility of obtaining capital can be an even bigger benefit than the tax advantages, and for this the Cayman Islands are well renowned as a hotspot for Chinese capital.

PFIC Issues

Foreign corporations can be considered passive foreign investment companies (i.e., mutual funds) if they own an average of more than 50% passive income producing assets, or more than 75% of the gross income is passive-type income. Keep in mind that cash reserves earning interest are considered income-producing assets. This is important because when a corporation is deemed a PFIC, there are additional tax law rules that come into play when income is distributed, including penalty taxes for certain income.

There is an overlap rule where a CFC that is also considered a PFIC will not need to file Form 8621 because they already are required to file Form 5471 to report this income. However, in some circumstances it can be beneficial to file Form 8621 to elect the qualified electing fund (QEF) or Mark to Market (MTM) treatment, as explained in Chapter 5, giving a tax-planning opportunity here. Using the QEF treatment, the income from the CFC can be reported as long-term capital gains, but the CFC must provide the necessary documentation to elect this.

The MTM income is still considered ordinary income, and there is a risk here if more than one U.S. taxpayer owns the CFC as the taxes paid annually by one taxpayer will be allocated to all taxpayers on the year of distribution from the CFC. This means that if you and your buddy own a CFC together, and only you file Form 8621 and pay tax on MTM basis, then the corporation distributes the fund, your buddy gets half of the credit for the tax you paid, and you pay tax a second time on half the income.

This only applies to CFCs, so for corporations that fall into the PFIC category with less than 50% U.S. ownership, the U.S. taxpayer may be required to file Form 8621, even if there is no 5471 filing requirement. Even if not required, taxpayers in this situation may want to file Form 8621 to choose the QEF or M2M treatments as discussed above.

Another issue with this is "once a PFIC, always a PFIC." Thus, in the past, certain hedge funds have been burned with investments in startup companies where the first year they held large amounts of cash, earning PFIC status. This situation is also a particular issue to oil and gas drilling companies.

Penalties for Not Filing or Incorrectly Filing

Form 5471 falls under the FATCA requirements for reporting foreign accounts. Therefore the penalties for not filing this return timely, or filing incorrectly, is just as tough as other FATCA-related penalties.

There is a $10,000 penalty for failing to file Form 5471 or filing late. These penalties used to be very selectively applied, but the IRS now automatically imposes this. If the IRS requests for you to file Form 5471, and you fail to do so, then 90 days later they can assess an additional $10,000 penalty. After this, each 30-day period results in an additional penalty, until the maximum penalty of $50,000 is reached.

In addition to this penalty, the foreign taxes allowable to offset any U.S. income tax due are reduced by 10%. This jumps up 90 days later, similar to the failure-to-file penalty, to being an additional 5% of the the tax calculated for each three-month period, or $10,000—whichever is greater. This means that even if you don't have tax to deduct against your income, you could end up with an additional $10,000 penalty here.

The final penalty is a 40% accuracy penalty that can be assessed for any underpayment of tax. I have summed all these penalties up in the following chart:

Form 5471 & 8865 Penalties:

$10,000 failure-to-file penalty, automatically imposed for each LATE OR MISSING 5471.

90 days after requested by IRS, additional $10,000 penalty for each 30 DAYS late—up to a total of $50,000.

Plus 10% REDUCTION OF FOREIGN TAXES available to offset U.S. tax under IRC § 901, 902 and 960.

90 days after, requested deductible taxes are reduced 5% more for each 3 months up TO THE GREATER OF $10,000 or the total amount of tax.

40% ACCURACY-RELATED PENALTY can also be assessed for underpayment of tax.

It is important to note that these penalties can be assessed even if you file a timely Form 5471 if you don't include the required statements or make other errors in your preparation. This is a good reason to never self-prepare this form. I actually recommend that tax professionals don't even prepare Form 5471 —unless they are experienced with business returns and willing to invest the hours to learn it correctly.

Statute of Limitations

Another area where you run risk with Form 5471 is with regard to the statute of limitations, which is open indefinitely when required information has not been properly reported. After filing, the statute remains open for three years past the normal statute for the forms you are filing. And if this is reopened, it opens all areas of the return up for audit.

Filing Exceptions

Not everyone who owns part of a foreign corporation needs to file informational returns on behalf of that corporation. In general, less than 10% constructive ownership means you will not need to file Form 5471. But constructive ownership is a little bit confusing of a concept. This can mean ownership through other entities. It also can include ownership by a non-resident alien spouse or other close family members such as children. However, if you really do own less than 10% of the company and your family is not involved, you safely cannot file Form 5471.

Also, if another U.S. shareholder files Form 5471 attached to their return and names you in it, then you do not need to file Form 5471. However, it is still recommended you attach a statement to your return explaining the situation. It is also recommended that the owner with the largest percentage of ownership attach the return to his or her return. This should be done consistently; it is best practice to try and maintain the same filing patterns between years whenever possible.

If you don't directly own stock in the company, but you would be considered a shareholder only because of attribution rules from a non-resident alien spouse or family member, then you also don't need to file. Still, in many cases there are family trusts or partnerships that may own interest in the company, and this makes it far more complex to determine ownership. Ownership through these entities is still considered constructive ownership.

One last situation that doesn't require annual filing is if your ownership is constructively less than 50% and you meet the other requirements as a Category 2-only filer, then you only need to file in years you acquire or dispose of interest in the company.

Dormant Foreign Corporations

Dormant foreign corporations are able to file an abbreviated Form 5471, only needing the first page filed. To determine if the company is dormant, it must meet ALL of the following requirements:

1. The corporation received or accrued no more than $5,000 in income.

2. The corporation paid or accrued no more than $5,000 in expenses.

3. The value of assets (gross amounts not net any liabilities such as a mortgage) are less than $100,000, calculated using GAAP.

4. No shares in the corporation were sold, disposed of, redeemed, exchanged, or transferred and the corporation was not part of a reorganization.

5. No assets were sold, exchanged, redeemed, or transferred in excess of $5,000 value.

6. Changes to accumulated earnings and profit were only due to income or expenses over $5,000.

7. No distributions were made to shareholders.

8. The corporation owned no stock in other corporations, except for other dormant foreign corporations.

Foreign corporations filing the abbreviated one-page dormant corporation form should be sure to keep good books and records because if the IRS requests documentation to prove this status, only 90 days are given to provide this information. The steep penalties for not filing Form 5471 and loss of foreign tax credit can be applied if this information is not provided within that short 90-day window.

Filing Requirements

To determine what you will need to file, you must first determine which category you fall under. These categories are listed on the front page of Form 5471 and define everything from what is taxable income to which schedules need to be included with the return. This can be a confusing issue, so it is best to obtain professional help if you are confused.

The instructions of form 5471 must be carefully read to understand which category of filer one is. Typically, filers will fall under either categories 4 and 5, or 2 and 3, but it can be any combination and often is all four in a year of acquisition.

Attribution Rules

When there is a family business, there is risk that the ownership of the company by the U.S. taxpayer could be much greater under U.S. tax law than what is

Filing Requirements for Categories of Filers

Required Information*	Category of Filer				
	1	2	3	4	5
The identifying information on page 1 of Form 5471 above Schedule A, see **Specific Instructions**		√	√	√	√
Schedule A			√	√	
Schedule B			√	√	
Schedules C, E, and F			√	√	
Schedule G		√	√	√	√
Schedule H				√	√
Schedule I				√	√
Separate Schedule J				√	√
Separate Schedule M				√	
Separate Schedule O, Part I	√				
Separate Schedule O, Part II		√			

*See also Additional Filing Requirements on page 3.

apparent at first glance. If a close family member such as a spouse or parent owns stock in the company, then the percentage of ownership is increased from the attribution rules. For example, if a non-resident alien husband owns 50% of a company and his spouse owns 10%, she is still a category 4 filer that is required to file a tax return every year, even though her percentage is so low that at first glance one would think she is not required to file at all.

However, the attribution rules do not by themselves require a taxpayer to file. If one does not own direct or indirect interest in the foreign corporation, then Form 5471 would only be required to be filed because of constructive ownership from a non-resident alien spouse.

Controlled Foreign Corporation

It is important be able to determine if your company is a controlled foreign corporation, or CFC, because of how Subpart F income works. To be considered a CFC, you must have U.S. ownership of 51% or greater. This must be actual, direct ownership by U.S. citizens; ownership via the attribution rules does not count in calculating the percentage to determine if a company is a CFC.

CFCs with passive income or income for personal services may have Subpart F income when dividends are not distributed. If you have a CFC and your company is making a decent profit, it is highly recommended that you pay yourself wages. This is similar to Subchapter S corporations within the United States, that without paying wages out to the primary owners, the dividends these companies pay start to look fishy. Well, with foreign corporations, it is not paying dividends or wages that looks fishy.

> **Triggers for Subpart F Income:**
> - Foreign personal holding company (investment) income (I.R.C. Section 954(c))
> - Foreign-base company sales (to U.S. persons/entities) income (I.R.C Section 954(d))
> - Foreign-base personal services income (I.R.C. Section 954(e))
> - Insurance income (I.R.C Section 953);
> - Income from countries subject to international boycotts (I.R.C. Section 999);
> - Illegal bribes, kickbacks, and other similar payments (I.R.C. Section 162 (c)); and
> - Income from countries where the United States has severed diplomatic relations (I.R.C. Section 901 (j)).
> - Foreign-base company shipping (I.R.C Section 954 ((f)) and oil related income (I.R.C. Section 954 (g))

In some instances, Subpart F income is most beneficial. Subpart F income is generally not subject to Net Investment Income Tax (NIIT) unless it is Previously Taxable Income (PTI). If you have PTI subject to NIIT, you may want to make the election under Reg. § 1411-10(g) to treat all Subpart F income subject to NIIT to not have to break it out separately. Better yet, if you are in a tax-treaty country, pay yourself a dividend that will be treated as a qualified dividend and taxed at lower rates.

Subpart F losses can also be beneficial, and it can be treated much like how S corporation income and expenses are treated. One item to be careful about though, is that loans to shareholders may be considered Subpart F income. This is stricter than how S corporations work, and can make it a bit more challenging to make the equity and debt sides of the balance sheet match up.

There is a "de minimus" rule that exempts U.S. shareholders from reporting small amounts of Subpart F income. In general, if the income that would be subject to Subpart F is less than one million dollars or less than 5% of the gross income, it is exempted. Also, investment income that is less than 5% of gross income is exempted.

Foreign Partnership Returns

Foreign partnerships are filed on Form 8865, and as the forms are a bit more straightforward than working with Form 5471, I will touch here just on some of the essentials, such as understanding the categories of filers. This is determined using the same attribution and constructive ownership rules as with foreign corporations.

> **Form 8865 Categories of Filers:**
> • "Category 1" is a U.S. person who controls a foreign partnership.
> • "Category 2" is a U.S. person owning at least 10% of a foreign partnership controlled by U.S. persons, each owning minimum 10% interest.
> • "Category 3" is a U.S. person who contributes property to a foreign partnership.
> • "Category 4" applies to acquisitions, dispositions, or changes in proportionate interest that cause a 10% increase or a 10% decrease in the partnership interest.

Delinquent Submission Procedures

The IRS has been gracious enough to offer an amnesty program for getting caught up with filing missing informational returns. http://www.irs.gov/Individuals/International-Taxpayers/Delinquent-International-Information-Return-Submission-Procedures.

Repatriation Tax

The Tax Cuts and Jobs Act both lowered the corporate tax rate to 21% and, in a great show of additional corporate generosity, added a section on repatriating income at tax rates as low as 8%, and this tax can be paid over eight years with no interest. This has both advantages and disadvantages, as this low rate can be good if you want to bring funds in, but it cannot be offset by foreign tax credit, so it penalizes companies operating in high-tax jurisdictions.

With this being a forced repatriation, it hits hard on some companies that have high retained earnings, but can be beneficial to other companies that want to bring profits held in tax-free jurisdictions to the United States.

The repatriation only applies to CFCs, so if there is less than 51% U.S. ownership, this does not apply. Also, if Subpart F income applies, then the income passes through at ordinary income rates and the repatriation tax also does not apply.

11. INITIAL COIN OFFERINGS

Initial coin offerings (ICOs) have changed the landscape of investments. ICOs fall on the spectrum in between crowdfunding and traditional initial public offerings of stocks. Not to be scoffed at, some ICOs have raised billions of dollars. However, many others raise modest amounts or raise some now and keep tokens for future raises.

The IRS has not come out with any guidance about the tax treatment of ICOs, so tax logic must be applied as best as possible. Considering tax law is far from logical, this is rather challenging.

The first item to consider is the type of token. Utility tokens are what most promoters of ICOs want their tokens to be considered, but this holds true in only certain cases. For a token to have a true utility, it must be essential to the project. In many cases, this means a token that can be exchanged for goods or services. Ethereum is the gold standard example of a utility token.

This compares with standard cryptocurrency offerings such as Bitcoin, Litecoin, or Bitcoin Cash, where the true intention was to create a token that can be used as payment in lieu of government-issued currency. Even though Ethereum is now used as a cryptocurrency in many instances, if you read the original white paper, it is clear that the intention was to have the token serve a utility purpose.

Other token offerings have come out in the last year, including security token offerings (STOs) that are tokenizing the equity from a company and selling in a token sale. JOBS Cryptocurrency Offerings (JCOs) are a hybrid where a security token is issued that is later convertible to a utility token. And initial loan procurement (ILP) token offerings are a hybrid way of issuing debt in a tokenized form.

Money Equivalents

Cryptocurrencies that are intended to be used as a monetary equivalent are fully taxable when sold. Any business expenses related to development or production of the cryptocurrency is deductible against the income, just like with mining. If a company issuing a fungible cryptocurrency retains coins to sell at a later date in order to raise more funds, then these retained coins are only taxable once they are sold.

Tokenizing Business

Utility tokens, when issued, are generally taxable income under U.S. law. An easy way to think about it is if you were offering a product for sale using a crowdfunding platform such as Kickstarter, then the pre-sale of goods when you receive the funds is considered income. A token sale is essentially a pre-sale of goods or services, and as such it is fairly clear to draw the line that this is taxable income.

Managing this potential tax burden requires careful planning. One could draw a conclusion that utility tokens could be considered equivalent to gift cards, and as such, revenue ruling 2004-34 allows for a procedure of deferring a portion of the income to the following tax year. Combining this with a carefully determined fiscal year can provide up to two full years of using the funds toward development and marketing before the income becomes taxable for U.S. purposes.

Tokenized Securities

Typically, when you raise money by selling equity in a company, there is no taxable gain. It could be argued that issuing a security token is equivalent to selling shares but in a tokenized form, especially when the token holders are also given voting rights and a share of earnings. However, the tokens sold are property that can be traded and, as such, it could also be argued this is a sale of company-created property.

I would lean in the direction of considering this a sale of equity in most cases. JCOs would be a notable exception, as with the convertible properties to a utility token there would certainly be tax recognized at the time of the conversion to the utility token.

One of the issues with STOs and JCOs is that the funds raised for the company may still be determined income by the IRS, depending on the structure. There is no clear guidance yet regarding whether or not these products could be considered an equity investment that would be tax free when contributed to the company. Thus the murky tax position can lead to an excess amount of legal costs down the line if a position taken needs to be defended in the examination-and-appeals process.

Tokenized Loans

Borrowing money is not taxable to the borrower. The money borrowed only becomes taxable if the borrower defaults on the loan. As such, ILPs could become a tax-advantaged method of raising funds for companies issuing tokens in the future.

Dividends

As the STO industry is still so new, it is unclear how many companies are planning to handle informational reporting of dividends paid to token holders. What is clear is that with payments being made there will typically be some sort of requirement for reporting these payments, and collecting this information of who to issue this to may be a challenge as these tokens are re-sold on secondary markets.

Hopefully the exchanges that will service this industry will collect and remit this information to the issuing company in the way brokerage houses send this to companies that issued stock. But I wouldn't hold my breath, as with the high value placed on anonymity in the crypto world, many investors may be reluctant to provide this information.

Airdrops

Airdrops are when token sales distribute tokens in exchange for individuals and social influencers sharing their companies to their networks or otherwise endorsing them. While airdrops are not taxable to the company, these payments may require informational reporting. This is because it could be determined that these payments are for a service being performed, and as such all participants in an airdrop are independent contractors.

Under U.S. law, this means anyone paid over the equivalent of $600 must receive a Form 1099 reporting the amount of their payment. The trouble, though, is most companies are not collecting the information needed to issue this form come year end. When running an airdrop, you should be collecting a Form W-9 from every participant who would potentially receive more than this amount.

12. NON-RESIDENT TAX ISSUES

Those who are not U.S. citizens may also need to file U.S. tax returns if they have business, wage, or investment income in the United States and don't meet the residence guidelines,. In these cases, they must file Form 1040NR.

This is very important to investors of crypto projects or tokenized venture funds that fall under U.S. law, because if a U.S. company makes payments to a foreign person, there is a default backup withholding required by the company of 30% of the distribution! If the company does not withhold this from the distribution, the company is still on the hook for paying this, and can lead to a huge tax burden.

Part of the problem is the pseudonymity of the crypto space, and you may not know if the owners of tokens are foreign or not. I could see companies down the line (after facing tax and penalties for getting this wrong) withholding 30% across the board for any token holder who did not provide U.S. tax information. We are still early in the development of this industry and these financial products, so this has not happened yet, but I think this chapter on non-resident returns may be very helpful in the future to non-U.S. individuals who need this information, or for U.S. individuals who choose to expatriate, as afterward any U.S. income they receive will be filed on non-resident returns.

Tax Residency

Residency for tax purposes is not the same as for immigration purposes. Just because you are not a legal immigrant does not mean you don't have tax obligations still to the United States. Beyond those who have green cards or citizenship, there is a requirement that anyone who spent more than 183 days in the United States has a requirement to file tax returns as a full-year resident, with few exceptions.

Being a full-year U.S. resident means that you will be taxed on your worldwide income. For some, this is a non-issue, but for others this can be a huge bureaucratic nightmare, as well as being an expensive proposition. The calculation of dates for requirement to file is actually a bit more complex than just the 183-day rule. This is governed by the Substantial Presence Test:

> **Substantial Presence Test U.S. Dates:**
>
> \>30 days in current tax year AND
>
> \>183 days in most recent 3-year period:
>
> - all days year 1 (current)
> - ⅓ days year 2
> - ⅙ days year 3

To determine the dates you spent in the United States, you need to count every date from when you arrived on U.S. soil. Often this can be difficult to calculate, but luckily the Department of Homeland Security has a website where you can retrieve this information: https://i94.cbp.dhs.gov/I94/request.html.

Certain dates are not counted, such as days that meant less than 24 hours spent in the United

States ,such as cross-border commuting, shopping trips from residents of Canada or Mexico, or if you were only in the United States on a transfer for international travel. There is also a "de minimus" rule where trips of less than ten days can be excluded. Crew members of ships and workers of foreign governments on A-2 visas are also exempt. Teachers and students on F, J, M, or Q visas and professional athletes may file Form 8843 to claim exemption. There is also an exception for those who are unable to leave due to a medical condition.

For those who meet the Substantial Presence Test and do not meet the other exceptions, it is also possible to claim exemption from two other methods. One is using the "closer connection" exemption, but this is only available if the Substantial Presence Test was not met in the current tax year. The second method is using a tax treaty exception for those who are residents of treaty countries. Treaty exceptions are based on permanent home, area of vital interest, habitual abode, and nationality, and are generally contained in Article IV of the treaty.

Electing Treatment as a Resident Alien

If you would benefit from mortgage deduction or real-estate losses not allowed on a 1040NR return, you may qualify to be treated as a resident alien. You may elect this if you have been present in the United

States for at least 31 days in the tax year, then you must have continued to be present in the United States for at least 75% of the following days in the tax year, although five-day de minimus absences can be treated as U.S. time. Your spouse and dependents must also qualify to be able to make this election. This may also facilitate breaking ties with a former country—Canadian residents commonly do this when moving to the United States in order to have simplified tax treatment.

Start and End of Residency

If you do end up having residency in the United States or if you are ending your residency, it is important to know the actual starting and ending dates of residency, as this will be when a person must base their time as a resident on their tax return. For those who meet the Substantial Presence Test, the date is the first date you entered the United States, less any de minimus travels that were for less than ten days. If you receive a green card for the United States, then the first date you are considered a resident is the first day on U.S. soil with the green card. If your visa status has changed, it will be the first date with the new visa status. If it is more beneficial to be considered a full year resident for this first year, you can file an election to do so.

Effectively Connected Income

The main item of importance with non-resident returns to understand is the concept of effectively connected income (ECI). This refers to income that is from an active trade or business carried on within the United States. You may elect to have residential real estate treated as effectively connected income under a Sec 671(d) election.

Pension income from previously having worked in the United States is generally considered effectively connected income. However, Social Security income is considered not-effectively connected income and in most cases is subject to the 30% flat tax, although there are a few treaty exemptions to this.

U.S. Investment Income

Income from U.S. investments such as stocks and bonds are treated very differently for non-residents than for residents. Capital gains, except for the gains on real estate, are not taxable. This means that non-citizens can invest in U.S. securities and pay zero capital gains when they sell these equities. As with most rules though, there are exceptions to this one. The main exception is that if you are present in the United States for greater than 183 days in the tax year, then your U.S. source capital gains will be taxed at a flat 30% tax rate, or possibly a lower rate, depending on tax treaties.

Interest income, on the other hand, if from a US bank or similar institution and not connected with a US business activity, is tax-exempt. However, interest from other types of activities may be taxable, depending on how it is connected to U.S. business activities, as well as how it fits into the maze of treaty exceptions available.

Deductions Available

Itemized deductions differ for non-residents in that certain expenses, such as medical deductions and real estate taxes, are no longer included. Joint and Head of Household filing status are not available, and only in a few occasions may an exemption for dependents be taken.

Expatriation Tax

Expatriation tax is a bit of a misnomer. It does not apply automatically because of expatriation, and rarely actually applies to expatriates because of the income thresholds. However, if a U.S. resident ceases to be a resident, then becomes a U.S. resident again within the following three-year period. this tax can be triggered under special rules, requiring gains on property to be calculated in a Mark-to-Market fashion. Therefore expatriation tax is more likely to be an issue for non-citizens than for those who surrender citizenship, as backwards as that sounds.

Non-Resident Alien Investment in Companies

Foreign investment in U.S. companies or real estate is also an issue I am asked about quite often. It is common that expats will want to partner with a non-resident alien spouse or business partner they have met living abroad to go into a venture back in the United States. This has certain other issues with it that must be addressed.

Withholding Requirements

If you own a U.S. company and have investments from people who are not U.S. citizens or residents, you may need to withhold tax on their behalf if you pay them distributions based on business income. The general amount of withholding is 30%, and Form 1042 is filed to report this amount. The trouble is that, with tokenized investments, the tokens can be easily traded on secondary markets or even with peer-to-peer transfers, and these forms may not be reported properly.

A company may not even receive the information needed to know if the owner of the tokens is foreign, let alone the information to send out the required informational returns. This can be quite a problem for U.S.-based companies.

Obtaining ITIN

To do any business in the United States, one must have a tax ID number. Most non-resident aliens obtain this by filing Form W-7 to obtain an ITIN number. It used to be that once you received an ITIN, it was valid forever, but they changed this a couple years ago and now they are valid for only four years. The renewal process takes 14 weeks, so this must be planned for in advance of filing.

13. EXPATRIATION

Some high-profile members of the crypto community have expatriated to reduce their tax burden, the most notable being "Bitcoin Jesus" Roger Ver. This has held unexpected consequences for Mr. Ver, though, as he has repeatedly been denied visas to travel to crypto conventions in the United States after expatriation.

Depending on the location of the second passport, travel to the United States may or may not be restricted, so this is only a secondary concern. But just because you expatriate from the United States does not mean that you are eternally beyond the clutches of Uncle Sam. Any U.S.-sourced income is still subject to U.S. taxes, and if you spend over 183 days in the United States during a year, then you automatically become a resident alien and again fall under U.S. tax law. Thus you need to make sure that spending time in the United States is not going to be a future priority before expatriating.

As I mentioned in the first chapter, it has become increasingly common for people to renounce their U.S. citizenship. I see it far more often than I ever expected. Relinquishing of green cards is also common practice for many who are sick of both tax and informational return reporting requirements.

Expatriating for the specific purpose of avoiding U.S. taxation is not advisable. The Foreign Investors Tax Act reduced tax rates for non-resident aliens in order to encourage investment in the United States. In order to prevent U.S. citizens from abandoning citizenship for tax purposes, Congress passed Section 877 of the tax code. This is where the familiar idea of having to pay tax for five years after expatriation comes from. Contrary to popular belief, there is no standard expatriation tax such as this, a recurring U.S. resident tax liability is only generated when citizenship has been surrendered for tax purposes. Thus it is critical when expatriating to show business or personal reasons beyond avoidance of tax. There are exceptions to this, however, mainly with regard to treaty countries as expressed in the pivotal tax court case, Crow v. Commissioner, 85 T.C. 376, 380 (1985).

In order to expatriate, you must first be current on tax returns as the government will review your last five years' worth of tax returns. If you have not filed the five previous years' returns, you will fall under the "Covered Expatriate" rules and may be subject to an exit tax for all assets owned when expatriating. When you are ready, you will file Form I-407 to renounce citizenship, and that is what will define your date of expatriation.

For those who qualify for U.S. residency simply because of the Substantial Presence test, your residency ends in the year you cease being a resident. In general, December 31 is the date of the end of residency in this situation, and no dual-status return will need to be filed. However, there are exceptions to this, as with most areas of tax law, so you may want to consult with a professional. If you filed Form I-407, the date you filed this form is the date your citizenship ends.

Dual-Status Return

The final year of filing when expatriating or surrendering a green card it is often necessary to file what is known as a Dual-Status Tax Return. When acquiring a green card, citizenship, or residency in the United States, this also can be filed. This is made up of two tax returns—both the standard Form 1040 and a 1040NR. One of these forms will represent the status at the end of the year and be considered the "Dual Status Return"; the other form will then be attached as the "Dual Status Statement."

For example, when expatriating because at the end of the year you will be a non-resident, Form 1040NR is the "Dual Status Return" and attached to this is the Form 1040 as a "Dual Status Statement." This sounds very simple when I explain it, but most people have a hard time doing this correctly in practice, as typically the 1040 resident return will be the one with all income, deductions, and tax liability, and the 1040NR will essentially be blank.

It is possible when renouncing a green card to elect to be treated as a resident alien until the end of the tax year. This is often of benefit when filing jointly with a spouse as otherwise married filing separate status will need to be used, and this status is penalized by removing many credits and advantages of filing jointly. Generally in the dual-status reporting year, no FATCA reporting is required. However, if you choose to be treated as a resident alien for the remainder of the year, then the FBAR report and Form 8938 will still be required, if relevant. Head of Household filing status is not allowed during a dual-status filing year.

Form 8854

U.S. citizens and green card holders for longer than eight years must file Form 8854 when expatriating. Even if only one spouse is expatriating, if you filed jointly in previous years you will use the income numbers from your joint returns; this is not split or allocated. Whether your assets are split depends on the matrimonial regime in your country of residency. Either way, you will include all assets, including your primary residence.

It is recommended to prepare Form 8854 very close to the date of expatriation—this way it is easier to account for all assets and appraisals can be done, if needed. However, the form cannot be filed until the previous year, when it is attached to your final tax returns and the information transferred to the next year's form version at that time.

Covered Expatriates

Covered expatriates are taxpayers that have either taxable income higher than $160,000 averaged over the last five years, or a net worth of over two million dollars when they expatriated. You can also fall into the covered expatriate boat if you haven't filed the last five years' worth of tax returns or if you have deferred compensation or a non-grantor trust. Dual citizens who have not lived in the United States for longer than ten years or who expatriated before age 18½ can have higher income and net worths and not be considered covered expatriates.

Why do you not want to be considered a covered expatriate? Because covered expatriates are subject to an exit tax based on the Mark-to-Market rules. This means the IRS will treat everything you owned on the day you expatriated as if it was sold, and you will be taxed on the value of all assets owned at that time with one exception—you have a $690,000 reduction of your taxable net gain. Still, you can end up with quite a high tax bill from this, and asset values are hotly debated at this point.

If your assets are close in value to the $2 million benchmark amount, it is wise to have professional appraisals done on all your assets; this way there is documentation of the value at time of expatriation.

Filing After Expatriation

Contrary to popular belief, it is not necessary for most taxpayers to continue filing U.S. tax returns after expatriation. This includes both covered and non-covered expatriates. What generates a requirement to continue filing U.S. tax returns is when a covered expatriate has a deferred compensation pension plan and opted to pay tax gradually on this amount after expatriation. By doing this, they also forfeit any treaty benefits that otherwise would reduce tax on their pension distributions.

14. Crypto Asset Reporting Requirements

The biggest risk tax-wise that I would say most cryptocurrency investors have and overlook, or get wrong, is the requirements to report crypto holdings on FBAR reports and Form 8938. Considering that no tax is generated from these filings, and that the penalties are a minimum of $10,000 a year for not filing or underreporting, the risk is high for making mistakes, but the cost of complying is miniscule. Thus there really is no excuse to get this wrong, except that many people do just because they don't have the correct information. It really is terrible how much misinformation is out there. I even saw a *Forbes* article once from a prominent tax writer who I will not name, who wrote that crypto accounts don't need to be reported. What terrible advice! It really is easy to protect yourself in this area, and doesn't take a lot of time to prepare the forms, which are mostly just reporting the highest balances of various accounts.

The FATCA act that came into law in March of 2010 certainly made life more difficult for Americans living abroad. However, the legislation this act is based on has been on the books for far longer. Starting in 1970, when the Bank Secrecy Act was passed, there became a governmental trend to seek out assets hidden by money laundering and wealthy individuals attempting tax evasion. Unfortunately though, the law is far broader reaching than just affecting the 1% and the overtly illegal enterprises it was intended to target. Now it causes many reporting and taxation headaches for U.S. expats across the globe, ranging from frozen assets abroad to U.S. banks refusing to issue accounts to foreign residents.

Cryptocurrency investments add an additional layer of complexity. This is because, depending on many details such as how they are held and where the company is formed, the token held may or may not be considered a foreign financial account. Cryptocurrency held in exchanges are foreign if held in a non-U.S. exchange. This is pretty simple. If you hold your crypto investments in an exchange like Coinbase, Kraken, or Robinhood, then you do not need to report these as foreign accounts and these amounts do not count toward the FBAR and 8938 thresholds. However, if you hold funds in foreign exchanges such as Binance, Poloniex, or Bitbay, then you will need to report the highest balances of these accounts once the thresholds are met.

Direct holdings in Bitcoin, Ethereum, or other cryptocurrencies in a wallet are not quite so straightforward. The tokens are considered to be an account of where they are held. So if you keep it on a flash drive in a safety deposit box, it is a U.S. account, but if you take it in your pocket traveling around the world, an argument could be made that this is a foreign account. If you live abroad and keep cold storage coins, then these coins are subject to the foreign bank account rules for reporting.

I would suspect that someday there may be further clarification on this by the IRS that will change which tokens must be reported. In the meantime, though, it is safer to overreport than to risk underreporting. This is because there is no tax owed from filing these informational returns, but the penalties of not filing properly are monumental.

FBAR Reports

If you have a combined account balance for any one day in the year where your total non-U.S. financial accounts exceeded $10,000, then you have to file an FBAR report. This $10,000 threshold is the balance across all foreign accounts on the highest value day of the year.

One other trigger for reporting would be if you are applying for the Streamlined Procedure amnesty program, then you must report a full six years of FBAR reports, even for years where bank balances dropped below $10,000. Remember that this is a reporting requirement only, not a tax that will be calculated on the reported balances, so it is always safe to err on the cautious side and overreport rather than miss something that could get you into trouble down the line.

It is important to note that all accounts must be reported, even if the account had zero balance in it during the year—if it remains open it must be reported. Although there is a box to check if you do not know the balance of the account, I would use this sparingly. In practice, it is preferable to estimate an amount slightly higher than what your highest balance would have been. This doesn't leave the treasury thinking you are hiding assets, and as no tax is calculated on these informational returns, it is erring to caution to overreport slightly. The times when using the balance unknown check box is best reserved for circumstances when you genuinely do not have access to accounts. An example would be a former employer's account you were a signatory on.

Business Bank Accounts

In general, any business bank accounts where you are a signatory on the account must be reported on the FBAR report. This includes accounts for companies you worked at, even if you are not an owner of that company.

If you are an owner, and your percentage of ownership is 51% or more, then you do not report this account under the signatory account; it is instead reported as a personal account under either part II or III, depending if there are other owners of the account.

Delinquent FBAR Submission Procedure

If you are up to date with your U.S. income tax requirements but have not filed FBAR reports, there is a procedure for getting up to date without the risk of penalties. See http://www.irs.gov/Individuals/International-Taxpayers/Delinquent-FBAR-Submission-Procedures.

Form 8938

If Form 8938...

The classification of custodial accounts is a part of the 8938 that always gives me a chuckle when I look at the form. According to the 8938 instructions, only accounts held by the taxpayer for the benefit of others are considered custodial accounts. Conversely, accounts held for the benefit of others are grantor trusts, which are not reported on Form 8938 and the box only needs to be checked to inform the IRS this structure exists. Thus there is a logic error here, as any custodial accounts that could be reported in Part I of the 8938 could not exist.

What Accounts Are Included?

Many people may think "Foreign Bank Account Reporting" just applies to banks, however this is a bit of a misnomer as many different types of financial accounts are included on both FBAR reports and Form 8938. For example, cash values of foreign-issued life insurance must be listed both on the FBAR report and Form 8938. To add to confusion, some accounts are only included on one and not the other, like bank accounts you do not own but are a signatory on, which are only listed on the FBAR report and not on Form 8938, whereas foreign hedge fund accounts must be listed on Form 8938 and do not need to be included on the FBAR report.

Aside from the official requirements for which forms to file, something can be said about the benefits of including all reasonable accounts on both reports; this way there are no discrepancies between the IRS and Treasury. I still would not include signatory accounts on 8938, but aside from that, I generally will overreport and include additional accounts that are not needed to avoid the risk of possibly not including something that is required to be reported. The fines for not including accounts are just so high, it is better to be safe, so I am always on the conservative side for informational return reporting.

I have included the IRS charts on FBAR and 8938 filing requirements for convenience. But as the information in these charts is updated regularly, I would suggest checking on the most recent update before making determinations. You can view these at http://www.irs.gov/Businesses/Comparison-of-Form-8938-and-FBAR-Requirements.

Nuances

The U.S. Treasury year-end rate must be used on both FBAR reports and Form 8938. These can be found online at: http://www.fms.treas.gov/intn.html. While alternate rates are allowable by the IRS to be used in tax returns, the Treasury rate is the required rate for FATCA reporting. The fact that Form 8938 gives you an option of listing an alternate source confuses many taxpayers into thinking they can use alternate exchange rate sources such as the IRS table rate or rates from a currency exchange such as OANDA, but this is not accurate. If no published rate is available, you can use an alternate rate, but you must disclose this on Form 8938.

Special Circumstances

If you apply for an ITIN number and elect to treat your non-resident alien spouse as a U.S. resident for tax purposes, your spouse's assets are not required to be reported on an FBAR report. However, if you are subject to filing Form 8938, your spouse's assets must be listed on this form. Therefore if you have 8938 filing requirements, it is recommended to file an FBAR report listing your spouse's assets; this way there is no discrepancy between what is reported to the Treasury Department and the IRS. Simple things like this will save you having to answer IRS questions down the line, so it's better to over-report now and save yourself from further scrutiny whenever possible.

15. GETTING CAUGHT UP

Many taxpayers have unwittingly been in violation of U.S. tax and bank reporting laws and only with recent media coverage has this been brought into the spotlight, causing many to seek help with getting caught up. Luckily, the IRS has made it relatively easy and inexpensive for taxpayers to get caught up and have a "clean slate" of sorts to start with.

Compliance Options

There are three main ways to submit delinquent tax and informational returns for U.S. citizens:

delinquent FBAR and informational return submission procedures for tax-compliant accounts, streamlined procedures for non-willful cases, and the offshore voluntary disclosure program (OVDP) for willful actors. Many people talk about "quiet disclosure" and just sending in returns, but this isn't recommended. If you don't have tax-compliant accounts and you send in FBARs and amended returns hoping nothing happens, that is taking a huge risk! While it is true that the IRS hasn't assessed penalties often with quiet disclosures, the IRS has strongly recommended against quiet disclosures. The truth is right now they have an easy way to identify this, and have already informed in certain reports that they know who these taxpayers are. With this in mind, I would not recommend that route.

I will explain these choices in more detail below, but the final decision of which method of filing is best will be in your hands. It will depend on your risk tolerance and financial situation. Some non-willful clients prefer OVDP for the closing agreement that protects them from any potential criminal issues and just lets them sleep better at night.

delinquent FBAR submission procedures	non-willful already tax-compliant	0% Penalty
delinquent informational return submission procedures	Non-Willful Already Tax-Compliant	0% Penalty
Streamlined Procedure Foreign	Foreign Resident Non-Willful Non-Compliant	0% Penalty
Streamlined Procedure Domestic	U.S. Resident Non-Willful Non-Compliant	5% Penalty
OVDP	Willful	27.5%-50% Penalty

With the many cases I have seen of clients not aware they even were U.S. citizens, let alone needed to file informational returns about their financial accounts, I don't see it being hard to draw non-willful conclusions with most of the cases I see. Also, many people moved to foreign countries and didn't realize that their U.S. tax obligations would continue even though they live in a new country where they must now file tax returns, or moved to a tax-free country and forgot all about taxes. Therefore, there are many instances where this failure to report tax and informational returns were inadvert and non-willful in nature.

I tend to advise against quiet disclosure, which means just filing the past due informational returns, in all cases. There are better options available now with the Delinquent FBAR Submission Procedures and Delinquent Informational Return Submission Procedures.

The main thing is to become compliant as quickly as possible, before IRS contact that would limit options. I've had clients start out using quiet disclosure or the Delinquent Informational Return Submission Procedures that end up going Streamlined after discovering they had more non-U.S. account assets than initially they imagined. And I have had streamlined clients switch back to one of the other options when it is discovered that they only actually had reporting requirements for a couple years and were barely at the minimum. Every case is different and risk must be carefully weighed out against the desired result and the cost to the client.

Your most advantageous option depends on the level of assets. If your non-filing is inadvertent in nature, and the amount is not much greater than $10,000, the likelihood of becoming compliant by simply filing six years of back FBAR reports in the Delinquent FBAR Submission Program is very high and this situation is easy to rectify, and inexpensive to file. If you have higher balances, and especially if you also would be required to file Form 8938 or report income from a foreign trust or corporation, you should apply for the Streamlined Procedure program. Only if your actions were willful should you apply for OVDP.

Streamlined Foreign Offshore

This is perhaps the best tax deal available right now. By filing three years of tax returns and six years of FBAR reports, you can have the proverbial slate wiped clean and pay zero penalties; only the tax is owed. In order to qualify, you must have not lived in the United States for at least one of the last 3 years, meaning you spent at least 330 days in the calendar year outside of the United States and territories— including Puerto Rico.

Streamlined Domestic Offshore

Unfortunately, the changes in the rules have made the streamlined domestic offshore procedure nearly useless now. This program is only available for domestic filers that have tax returns up to date already. However, the Delinquent FBAR and Informational return procedures already give an ability to do this without generating any penalties, whereas the streamlined domestic offshore calculates a 5% penalty on one year of foreign bank balances. This does not provide the statute of limitation protection or other protection beyond what the delinquent filing process provides. Thus, this is not an advantageous filing method any longer.

For U.S. resident taxpayers who are behind on both tax returns and informational reporting requirements, there is no easy way to become compliant any longer. The only remaining options are quiet disclosure and OVDP, the former with a reasonable amount of risk and the latter with very high costs.

Delinquent FBAR Submission Procedures

If you do not have assets in the range where there is significant risk of penalties and do not have income on your tax returns where you will face penalties, it may not be worthwhile to go through the Streamlined program and have your returns undergo significant scrutiny. Plus, the fees for filing are much higher in this case. Some people, though, are more conservative and prefer to file streamlined even when they have assets just above the $10k mark and zero-balance-due returns. The benefit of putting a stop to the statute of limitations at the three-year mark for tax returns is often appealing enough to warrant streamlined filing without any other risk factors. I always leave the choice up to the client and explain the options.

If you have filed tax returns timely and not included all of what is necessary, your prior tax preparer may actually have liability for not asking you the questions that would lead to including the right informational documents with your return. You could have recourse for any penalties incurred, if assessed. This is a good reason all tax professionals should ask every client if they have any non-U.S. financial accounts, although in practice few will.

If you have an account at a bank that has made disclosure agreements after the fact with Treasury or DOJ, then you may want to lean toward a more conservative position. Actually, in this case, you should disclose as loudly and with as much protection as possible. Every case is different.

It is still premature to say that the IRS is coming for every US citizen who has lived in a foreign country all their adult lives, and perhaps has a few retirement accounts with high dollar values.

The IRS does not have the manpower to answer the phone in a timely manner, and they offer practically no assistance to those who are trying to fully comply.

Offshore Voluntary Disclosure Program

Applying through the OVDP program is the only program that will waive criminal charges for willful cases. While avoiding jail time is likely worth however much it costs, this is an expensive program to apply to both for legal costs to apply and in the penalties assessed, which range from 27.5% to 50%

of the balances of unreported assets. This is just the tip of the iceberg, however. If there is unreported income, prepare to get dinged again, as the IRS will calculate penalties on the gross amount, not on any gain. So if you had $100,000 in stock that you paid $80,000 for initially, you will have to pay a penalty on the full $100,000 rather than on the $20,000 worth of capital gains.

While the quiet disclosure program carries risk, these penalties are guaranteed. So although I cannot conscionably recommend quiet disclosure, at the same time if nothing was done willfully, it may be the better option for U.S. residents that do not qualify for the other programs. Although the Delinquent FBAR and Informational return programs will cover nearly all taxpayers now.

There are two main reasons I prefer Streamlined Procedure or the Delinquent Informational Return Programs. 1. These rules are to find the shady people who have hidden money overseas, usually because of their shady activities. My clients are not the ones the IRS or Treasury has been looking for, they are mainly hardworking expats that have either had great careers or built successful businesses overseas. 2. There are no guarantees that even with all the work going into OVDP that it will be accepted. In the OVDP Instructions, it clearly states that the IRS goes over the entire submission with a fine-toothed comb and reserves the right to audit

	Form 8938	FBAR Report
Cryptocurrencies held in US brokerage accounts	No	No
Cryptocurrencies or other financial accounts held at foreign financial institutions	Yes	Yes
Cryptocurrencies held individually	No, unless assets held outside the U.S.	No, unless assets held outside the U.S.
Financial account held at a foreign branch of a U.S. financial institution	No	Yes
Financial account held at a U.S. branch of a foreign financial institution	No	No
Foreign financial account for which you have signature authority	No, unless you otherwise have an interest in the account.	Yes, subject to exceptions
Foreign stock or securities held in a financial account at a foreign financial institution	The account itself is subject to reporting, but contents not separately reported	The account itself is subject to reporting, but contents not separately reported
Foreign stock or securities not held in a financial account	Yes	No
Foreign partnership interests	Yes	No
Indirect interests in foreign financial assets through an entity	No	Yes, if sufficient ownership or beneficial interest in the entity.
Foreign mutual funds	Yes	Yes
Domestic mutual fund investing in foreign stocks and securities	No	No
Foreign accounts and foreign non-account investment assets held by foreign or domestic grantor trust for which you are the grantor	Yes, as to both foreign accounts and foreign non-account investment assets	Yes, as to foreign accounts
Foreign-issued life insurance or annuity contract with a cash-value	Yes	Yes
Foreign hedge funds and foreign private equity funds	Yes	No
Foreign real estate held directly	No	No
Foreign currency held directly	No	No
Precious Metals held directly	No	No
Personal property, held directly, such as art, antiques, jewelry, cars and other collectibles	No	No
Social Security'- type program benefits provided by a foreign government	No	No

Page 173

and/or reject it. The savings in potential penalties and risk better be worth it to go through that kind of ordeal.

Many attorneys, in my opinion, are too quick to recommend OVDP to their clients. In addition to lawyers leaning on the conservative side, OVDP also is the highest-fee avenue, and at times I have questioned if that is the motive. Due to the fees and the penalties assessed, this should only be used in willful cases where the protection from criminal prosecution is worth every penny. However, I have seen many clients with half-finished OVDP cases that were advised into this when they had no willful aspects to their case. I've had good luck in the past switching clients from OVDP to Streamlined Procedure. All the representation cases I have seen on this issue have involved me working with a panicked taxpayer and an IRS employee looking for simple tax and informational returns to be filed, so they can close a case and remove someone from their OVDP case list.

16. IRS PASSPORT REVOCATION

You're not going to enjoy the crypto islands very much unless you have a passport to get there. Thus the power of the IRS to revoke passports of delinquent tax filers is a terrifying proposition. This alone may be driving certain individuals to seek second-passport status in another country. Many Caribbean Islands offer attractive passport incentives to lure wealthy investors. But you still need a passport to get there in the first place.

Certainly the Internal Revenue Service is not

known to be a kind and understanding agency. However, my personal experience has been that most individual agents are helpful, or at least will be nice and civil if you treat them in a professional manner. There are several issues at play here, though. Much of how you will be treated is dependent on how well organized you are, and if you can show a knowledge of tax law.

There are certainly gray areas. It is a lot of work to put together a case with showing court precedents and interpretations to determine the risks of litigation. But if you are pushing into those gray areas, that is exactly what needs to be done.

The IRS has many devices they use for collections, including placing liens on property or even levying a bank account. But the new area that has many international clients up in arms is the ability of the IRS to enforce collections by revoking the passports of U.S. Citizens.

Passport Revocation

In the 2015 Fixing America's Surface Transportation (FAST) bill, Congress slipped in a provision that allows the IRS to revoke the passports of any taxpayer who is delinquent in taxes above a certain amount, starting at $50,000. While, as of this writing, the IRS has yet to revoke any passports, I am certain it is only a matter of time before they begin using this to enforce taxes due from American Citizens living abroad.

The calculation of taxes for allowing passport revocation is based on the total owed, including penalties and interest. Thus this can quickly add up, especially for taxpayers who have been penalized for not meeting reporting requirements for foreign corporations. However, the FBAR Penalty is specifically excluded from this amount, so any penalties relating to FBAR should not be included to reach this threshold. For 2018, the minimum amount for requesting revocation is $51,000.

The IRS will not directly revoke the passport. They will need to request that the State Department do this. Thus there will need to be notifications made to the taxpayer, and when this notification is received, there are options available about how to fight this. The State Department will also hold an application for 90 days with a revocation request to give time to resolve if there are any issues that the individual was unaware of.

Constitutional Rights

Kent v. Dules, a 1958 Supreme Court case, determined that the right to travel abroad is a liberty protected by the 5th Amendment and, as such, a passport cannot be taken away without due process. Therefore, if the IRS does send you notification that they are wanting to revoke your passport, you have the right to ask for a Collection Due Process hearing in tax court, and you can not only request that they show this is valid, but you also can put the burden on them to show there have been no procedures violated, per the IRS's taxpayer bill of rights. The State Department, however, is granted immunity with regard to this, so there is no way to resolve this legally against them.

Don't believe anyone, though, who may say that revoking a U.S. passport for tax purposes violates the 5th Amendment as a generalized statement. There was another landmark Supreme Court case in 2001, Weinstein v. Albright, where it was upheld that a person in arrears for child support payments could be denied a passport. The court will view owing of tax payments in a similar way, so as long as due process and administrative procedures are followed, the IRS does have the authority to revoke passports for tax delinquencies.

Staying Out of Trouble

There are several ways you can prevent the IRS from revoking your passport, even if you owe tax in excess of the amount deemed seriously delinquent. You can enter an installment agreement to pay off the debt over time. Or if that is unaffordable, an offer in compromise to either pay off a lump-sum lower amount, or a lower amount in payments, may be available. There are several options and all reach beyond the scope of this book. But if you are concerned about this, it is always best to seek help in advance of receiving a passport revocation notice, as more options are available at that time.

17. STATE TAX ISSUES

State taxes are another issue that is important to plan for. For expats, there are several distinct issues for taxes, the main one being residency and how it is determined. Each state has different rules, and it is important to research this carefully for your specific situation so as to not end up with very expensive problems.

Residency Rules

The most challenging aspect for state taxes is determining if you are still a resident in that state. In general, you must cut all ties with a state, such as getting rid of your driver's license, bank accounts, and mailing address, to be free from that state. Certain states have come out with safe-harbor rules in the last couple years that make it much easier to qualify as a non-resident than it used to be, but there are still some snags.

Civilian Contractors

If you are a civilian contractor in support of the U.S. military, then you are considered a full-year resident of the last state you lived in.

State Tax Guide

As it would take an encyclopedia set to fully cover state taxes, this chapter will be a quick introduction to the taxes in all states that affect expats. I will include some tips and traps I've run across in the field.

One thing to note is state standard deductions are often low. Although sometimes itemizing deductions on the federal return is not beneficial, on the state tax return it will be.

Same goes for the Foreign Earned Income Exclusion. If state residence is required, then often the Foreign Earned Income Exclusion will be more valuable overall than taking the foreign tax credit, even if the foreign tax credit removes all tax liability on the federal return. This can sometimes be a challenging decision to make between filing with the foreign tax credit and being able to receive a refundable child tax credit, or taking the Foreign Earned Income Exclusion to alleviate tax liability. The long-term position must also be examined in this situation.

It is good to keep in mind that state laws change frequently. For the most updated information, always verify before making any decisions based on state tax rules. Also, state law can be ambiguous at best, and often whether a position is legitimate or not is only clear after it has been tested.

Alabama

Residents of Alabama are still considered residents when accepting foreign positions, either for a temporary or permanent assignment. This is true even if a taxpayer has no property in Alabama after moving abroad. All income, wherever earned, is subject to Alabama tax as if a full-year physical resident.

Alabama personal income tax ranges from 2% to 5%. Social Security and many other qualified pensions are exempt from tax. There is no estate tax.

Alabama has a corporate tax of 6.5% of net income that is due in addition to the business privilege tax that all business entities must pay, which is based on net worth varying from $0.25 to $1.75 per every $1,000. There is a minimum tax of $100 and a maximum tax of $15,000 for most companies. Family-owned LLCs are capped at $500. Alabama tax information can be found at: http://revenue.alabama.gov/index.cfm.

Alaska

There is no personal income tax or inheritance tax in Alaska. Thus there is no taxation on expats who move abroad after living in this state.

There is a corporate income tax in Alaska ranging from 1% to 9.4%. The top income tax bracket comes in at a very low $90,000, possibly making this a state where domestic corporations are not the wisest entity structure unless really needed, or structured as an S-corp. LLCs and partnerships must file a biannual business report that costs $100 every two years to submit. Alaska tax information can be found at: http://www.revenue.state.ak.us. The business portal is at:http://commerce.alaska.gov/dnn/cbpl/Home.aspx.

Arizona

If moving abroad from Arizona for a temporary period, then you would still be considered a full-year resident and taxed on your worldwide income at the state level. But if your intention is to live overseas permanently, then you will no longer be considered a resident of Arizona upon moving.

Personal income taxes range from 2.59% to 4.54%, the highest rates starting around $150,000. Social Security is exempt, pensions are mostly fully taxable—the only exception being military and in-state pensions that have the first $2,500 of income treated as exempt. Arizona has no estate or gift tax.

Arizona has a corporate tax of 6.968%, with a $50 minimum tax. Most cities in Arizona also assess an annual privilege tax. Arizona tax information can be found at: http://www.azdor.gov/Home.aspx.

Arkansas

Arkansas is a domiciliary state and even if absent for a long period of time when living abroad, a taxpayer can still be deemed an Arkansas resident. This would make all income worldwide taxable in Arkansas.

Individual tax rates range from 1% to 7%, with the highest bracket coming in at a measly $34,000! The tax brackets and exemptions are so low, I've always wondered if someone at the Arkansas tax board confused real life values mixed with the prices on a Monopoly board.

Social Security is exempt, as is the first $6,000 of pension payments—including IRA distributions.

There are no estate taxes.

There is a corporate franchise tax that is figured based on stock issued of .3% of the outstanding capital stock or $150 minimum, $300 flat-rate for companies with no capital stock value. $150 flat-rate franchise tax for LLCs. Corporate tax rates range from 1% of the first $3,000 to 6.5% of any amount over $100,000. Arkansas does not conform to the federal depreciation rules regarding bonus depreciation, so care must be taken when deciding depreciation methods with Arkansas income. Tax and business information can be found at: http://www.state.ar.us/dfa.

California

While California is often villainized as a terrible state for expats, this is not entirely true. It can be a very tough state if one is still considered a resident as it does not allow for any Foreign Earned Income Exclusion to be claimed against income. This means California residents will often end up paying more state tax than federal if considered a resident. However, they have a "safe harbor" rule where if you are absent from California for 546 consecutive days, you can be considered a non-resident. This can be claimed from when you move abroad if your intent is to remain indefinitely in the foreign country where your employment contract is.

One of the most avaricious states with regard to enforcement, it is wise to file a non-resident tax return for a period after leaving the state and indefinitely if you receive any CA source income as marked on tax forms. As a default position, the Franchise Tax Board considers those who move out of the state still residents, and will hunt former residents down around the world to send tax bills.

Tax rates in the Golden State range from 1% to 13.3% in the top bracket—hope they give a lot of gold back for demanding that! Social Security benefits are exempt but all pensions are fully taxed. California also adds a 2.5% penalty tax on early distributions from pension funds. California has a refundable Child and Dependent Care Credit. There is no separate estate tax, just a minimal amount that piggy-backs off the federal.

California has sky-high business tax rates, with an $800 minimum tax for all business entities doing business in the state. Even a disregarded LLC holding a piece of real estate has to pay the $800 minimum tax annually. C-corps pay an 8.84% tax rate, S-corps pay a 1.5% tax rate, although financial corporations of either type pay even higher. LLCs are taxed at the corporate rate of 8.84% with the $800 minimum tax.

It is also important to note that some California cities have steep city tax rates based on gross receipts, often due even if the company reports a net loss. The city of Los Angeles has an income tax that varies based on the type of business, ranging from $1.01–$5.07 per $1,000 of gross income. San Francisco has flat taxes that range from $75 to $30,000, also based on total gross receipts. Additional tax information can be found at: https://www.ftb.ca.gov/index.shtml. The California business portal is at: http://www.sos.ca.gov/business.

Colorado

Colorado operates under the presumption that those who leave the state to work abroad are doing so on a temporary basis, thus they continue to consider them residents and subject to tax on a worldwide basis. This is because they have determined that most residents who leave, even for a long period of time, return eventually. Thus if you want to break ties with Colorado with a move overseas you must significantly document that this is a permanent move.

Tax rates assessed in Colorado are relatively straightforward—4.63% of federal adjusted taxable income. The first $20,000 of combined Social Security and pensions are deducted for those between 55–64 years of age, or $24,000 for those over 65. There is no estate tax in Colorado.

Corporations in Colorado pay a flat tax of 4.63% of net income, just like the personal taxes.

Partnerships and S-corps do not pay a separate tax but are required to withhold and pay in the 4.63% tax from partner or shareholder payments. State sales taxes are only 2.9% but in various localities they can range up to 9.6%. A periodic report accompanied by a $10 fee is due each year. Colorado business and tax information can be found at: http://www.colorado.gov.

Connecticut

Connecticut residents must be able to prove their move abroad is with the intent to reside there permanently in order to no longer be considered Connecticut residents. There was a case where a taxpayer was still considered a resident due to leasing his home rather than selling, and maintaining a country club membership. Thus these are the types of things the state will look at when making this determination.

Income tax rates range from 3% to 6.5%. Social Security is exempt for taxpayers with adjusted gross income under $50,000, or $60,000 if married. Half of military pensions are exempt, but all other out-of-state pensions are fully taxable. Connecticut has an estate tax starting at $2 million in assets at 7.2% and ranging up to 12% of total assets, making this a pretty expensive state to die in.

The Corporate tax rate is a 7.5% flat tax. Pass-through entities such as partnerships and S-corps are required to withhold tax on payments to partners or shareholders, if their share of Connecticut source income is $1,000 or more. Sales tax is 6.35%. There is a $250 annual business entity tax that must be paid by all S-corps, LLCs and limited partnerships. Connecticut tax information can be found at: http://www.ct.gov/drs/site/default.asp. Business registration is at: http://www.ct.gov/sots/site/default.asp.

Delaware

Delaware is similar to California where the default treatment is to consider taxpayers as residents when they move abroad, but they also offer a safe-harbor provision. The Delaware rules are that if your residence abroad is for longer than 495 days in any consecutive 18-month period, then you are considered a non-resident. You also cannot return to Delaware for more than 45 days within that period and cannot maintain a home in Delaware for your family.

Personal income tax rates range from 2.2% to 6.75%. Social Security and a portion of military pensions are exempt.

One of the more popular states for forming corporate entities, contrary to popular belief Delaware is not a tax-free state. Delaware charges an

8.7% flat rate tax on earnings attributed to the state. So why then are so many corporations headquartered there? Among other things, clearly written corporate business laws, especially with regard to mergers and acquisitions, attract businesses. Delaware does not tax their businesses on income that is earned in other states.

Delaware has a franchise tax that those who form companies there need to watch out for. If you do not assign a par value to your stock, or assign too high of par value, you can end up with sky-high franchise tax rates. Hearing of clients that got a $30,000 bill in the mail for their first franchise tax payment on a startup is not uncommon. Best to obtain legal counsel when forming in Delaware as it is a legally complex state, which is why it is so beloved by corporate lawyers. Delaware tax and business information can be found at: http://revenue.delaware.gov.

District of Columbia

DC considers anyone a resident who lives or keeps a home for their family in the district for at least 183 days out of the tax year. There is an exception for elected officials and their staffers who are domiciled in other states, and for people who do not have to file a U.S. tax return such as consulate staff.

Perhaps because the U.S. government is so close at hand, the state tax system is trying to out-complicate even its big brother, the IRS. DC's corporate tax law is full of credits and deductions for various types of businesses. Corporations are taxed at a flat 9.975%. Personal tax rates range from 4% to 8.95%. Social Security is exempted, as is the first $3,000 of military and government pensions.

DC even requires sole proprietorships and owners of rental properties to file a separate DC franchise tax return. This can be an added complexity for expat filers. For more information see: http://cfo.dc.gov.

Florida

There is no individual income tax in Florida, and as such is a non-issue for expats moving abroad. Also there is no estate tax in Florida. However there is a corporate tax: a flat 5.5%. Pass-through entities have no tax filing obligations although there is still an annual business reporting that is due: $138.75 for LLCs and $150 for corporations. Florida business portal can be viewed at: http://www.sunbiz.org.

Georgia

Residents of Georgia are considered to remain residents when moving abroad unless they can prove they have become a legal resident of another state. There is an exception if someone is not domiciled in

Georgia for more than 182 days within the tax year.

Personal income taxes range from 1% to 6%, the highest rate coming in at a whopping $7,000. There is no estate tax in Georgia.

Corporations are taxed at a flat 6% in addition to an annual $50 business form filing fee. Georgia has strong limited partnership laws where limited partners can still have some control over the business without losing their liability protection. This would be a desirable state to set up a limited partnership with a corporation as the general partner for that reason. Business information can be found at the secretary of state's site: http://sos.ga.gov/index.php. Tax information is at: https://etax.dor.ga.gov.

Hawaii

Hawaii residents moving abroad will be considered Hawaii residents unless permanent resident status is granted by the foreign country. Considered one of the highest tax states, at least for individuals, Hawaii's tax rates range from 1.4% to 11%. Estate taxes in Hawaii are especially thorny with the state taxing non-residents who own property here after the first $60,000! Non-resident estate tax rates run from 1.6%–8.4%. Residents have it a bit easier exemption wise; tax rates phase in between $3.5 million and $16 million, but the top rate is a whopping 16%. Definitely a state where estate planning is needed if you own much, especially as a non-resident.

Hawaii's corporate tax rates range from 4.5% to 6.4%, quite a bargain when compared to the individual income tax rates. Filing corporations in Hawaii is cheap and easy—$50 fee and an online portal that walks you through the process. The annual report filing fee is also a bargain, coming in at a bank-breaking $15. Only thing is then you own a corporation in Hawaii, not exactly a state where it is easy to get business or legal processes done in general, and the rather complex excise tax filings must be done at least bi-annually. Hawaii business registration can be found at: http://cca.hawaii.gov/breg. The department of taxation is at: http://tax.hawaii.gov.

Idaho

Taxpayers moving abroad from Idaho need merely to meet a three-prong intent test in order to establish non-residence:

1. Intent to abandon Idaho domicile.

2. Intent to acquire new domicile.

3. Physical presence in the new domicile.

Personal tax rates range from 1.6% to 7.4%. Idaho does not tax Social Security, and has many pension-related exemptions. There is no estate tax in

Idaho.

Corporate tax rates are a flat 7.4% and is a rather simple and straightforward tax system as both business and personal taxes in general conform to the federal law. There are no annual fees to pay when filing the annual reports. Business tax info is available at: http://tax.idaho.gov/i-1132.cfm. For forming businesses and annual report filing, please see: http://sos.idaho.gov.

Illinois

Expats from Illinois have it pretty easy. It is assumed that those who are absent a year or longer are non-residents of the state. However, those who leave on temporary assignments are still considered residents even if out of the state for longer than a year. The assumption goes the other direction as well. Anyone who lives at least nine months out of the tax year in Illinois is considered a resident of the state.

Personal tax rates are a flat 5%. Illinois does not tax distributions from any pension plans or Social Security, making it a good state to live in if you are going to convert an IRA to a Roth. Illinois does have an estate tax though, with a $4 million exemption.

Corporate taxes are a flat 9.5%, making S-corps and other pass-through entities look especially appealing in Illinois. Corporations must pay a $75 annual report fee, for LLCs this fee increases to $250 annually. Illinois tax information can be found at: http://www.revenue.state.il.us. The Illinois Secretary of State for annual filings is located at: http://www.cyberdriveillinois.com/home.html

Indiana

Indiana residence is not lost upon leaving the state to reside abroad unless the move is intended to be permanent. Individual tax rates are a flat 3.4%. Social Security tax is exempt and there is no inheritance tax.

Corporations pay a flat 7.5% and the annual filing fee for business entities is $20. More information on Indiana taxes can be found at: http://www.in.gov/dor/index.htm. Indiana business filing information is at: http://www.in.gov/sos/business/index.htm.

Iowa

Iowa does not have a definition for expatriate, however a clear procedure to renounce residency is available through the Julson ruling by meeting the following criteria:

1. Definite abandonment of former domicile.

2. Actual removal to, and physical presence in, the new domicile.

3. Bona fide intention to change and remain in this new domicile permanently or indefinitely.

Tax rates range from 0.36% to 8.98% with the highest bracket coming into play at $67,230. Active duty military pay is exempted. Social Security and pensions are taxed but a portion may receive an exemption. While not having an estate tax, if you inherit property while living in Iowa, you may face high taxes. The exemption is only $25,000 and the inheritance tax rates range from 1% to 15%.

For corporations, the tax rates range from 6% to 12%. A biennial report accompanied by a $45 fee must be filed. Iowa business and tax information can be found at: http://www.iowa.gov.

Kansas

Kansas does not have a clear definition for expatriates, and leaving the state for more than six months on a work assignment is not enough to relinquish residency. However, no set way to relinquish residency is stated. Luckily I have yet to see Kansas challenge any taxpayers on this, so the exact criteria that would apply remains a mystery. Tax rates range from 2.7% to 4.8% and are set to decrease each year for the next five years. Estate tax in Kansas has been repealed.

Corporations are taxed at 4% on the first $50,000 of income, then they pay 7% on income over that amount. Corporations and LLCs both pay a $55 annual filing fee. Kansas has a number of valuable tax credits for businesses, including an Angel Investor Credit of up to 50% of the amount of investment. More information on these credits can be seen at: http://www.ksrevenue.org/taxcredits.html. For business formations and annual reports, visit: https://www.kssos.org.

Kentucky

Kentucky presumes that a U.S. citizen who is no longer a U.S. resident retains Kentucky residence and files a Kentucky tax return as a resident. Income taxes range from 2% to 6%. Social Security and some pensions are exempt. Kentucky has an inheritance tax, but only if the proceeds are not going to immediate family members.

Corporate tax rates range from 4% to 6%. Pass-through entities are required to file a return and withhold tax on shareholder and partner payments, if tax liability appears to pass $500. There is an attractive tax credit for historic preservation available to business and real estate developers. Kentucky tax and business formation information can be found at: http://revenue.ky.gov.

Louisiana

Every person living in the state for at least six months during the year, or keeping a home for their family there, is considered a resident of Louisiana. However, change of domicile with the intent to make it a permanent move is allowable.

Personal tax rates range from 2–6%, with the top rate coming in at $50,000. Up to $6,000 of retirement income may be excluded. Social Security and most government pensions are excluded. School supplies for children and adults are a tax deduction, so save those back-to-school receipts.

Louisiana has high corporate tax rates ranging from 4% to 11%. In addition, a franchise tax based on capital runs at $1.50 for each $1,000 up to $300,000, then $3 per $1,000 above that. Louisiana tax information can be seen at: http://www.rev.state.la.us.

Maine

Maine has a foreign safe harbor that applies if an individual meets the following requirements:

1. Out of a 548-consecutive-day period, the taxpayer has been absent from Maine for at least 450 days.

2. During that 548-day period, the individual is not present in Maine for more than 90 days.

3. The taxpayer does not maintain a home for spouse or children who are present in the state for longer than 90 days.

Individual tax rates range from 2% to 7.95%, Estate tax ranges from 8% to 12% on amounts in excess of $2 million.

Corporate tax rates range from 3.5% to 8.93%. Maine has a number of business credits available for fringe benefits and community redevelopment projects, in addition to other activities such as visual media production and fishery infrastructure improvements. Plus, the Jobs and Investment Credit can cover many types of businesses. Definitely worth researching if doing business in Maine. More information can be found at: http://www.state.me.us/revenue/homepage.html.

Maryland

Maryland draws the line in the sand that even if a taxpayer's intent is to remain in a foreign country indefinitely, they cannot relinquish Maryland residency unless their visa is absent time restrictions. This is a tough criterion to get around unless you have dual citizenship or a spousal visa.

This state is also a bit complex tax-rate-wise for individual filers as not only does the state charge between 2% and 5.5%, but most of the 23 localities also charge residents between 1.15% and 3.15% as an income tax.

All businesses, including sole proprietors, if they own any depreciable assets, must register with the Department of Assessment and Taxation and file an annual personal property return. Corporate tax is a flat 8.25%. Maryland also has many business credits. Especially interesting to note are the fringe-benefit credits such as the commuting credit and the green development credits. More information on these business credits is at: http://taxes.marylandtaxes.com/Business_Taxes/General_Information/Business_Tax_Credits.

Massachusetts

Massachusetts bases residency determination on time spent within the state—183 days being the magic number. However, like California, it can be an expensive state if residency is determined as it does not allow the Foreign Earned Income Exclusion on a state level. It does have some credits though for income earned in Canada.

Individual taxes are a flat 5.5%. Social Security and many government pensions are considered exempt income. An estate tax is levied with $1 million as the exemption amount.

Corporate taxes are officially a flat 8%, but this is a bit misleading. Massachusetts has an excise tax in addition to the corporate income tax that is 9.5% of net income in addition to $2.60 per $1,000 of tangible property or net worth. The minimum excise tax is $456, plus add another $125 for filing your annual report. For LLCs there is a simpler but still relatively pricey annual filing fee of $500. Massachusetts has a voluntary disclosure program for businesses that have been engaging in business in the state but not filing taxes there that waives penalties, which is only valid if you are disclosing your income before receiving notification that you are in trouble. More information on all this can be found at: http://www.mass.gov/dor.

Michigan

Michigan has very specific criteria to meet for abandoning residence:

1. Specific intent to abandon old domicile.

2. Intent to acquire specific new domicile.

3. Actual physical presence in new domicile.

Personal tax rates are a flat 4.25% of federal AGI. Social Security and most pension income is exempt. Michigan currently does not collect an estate tax.

Corporate taxes are a flat 6%. In addition, the Single Business tax comes into pay for any business activity that earns over $350,000 in Michigan, including sales of real estate, real estate rental activities, and fees for personal services. This is a 1.9% tax that has several tax credits that can be applied toward it, but still adds up. More Michigan

tax information can be found at: http://
www.michigan.gov/taxes.

Minnesota

Minnesota allows non-residency to those who
spend 330 days outside of the United States during
any 12-month period, in essence to anyone meeting
the physical presence test of the Foreign Earned
Income Exclusion. They also allow the Foreign
Earned Income Exclusion to be taken by residents, so
they may just consider it to be too much hassle to
bother getting returns anymore once people qualify
for tax-free treatment.

Individual rates range from 5.35% to 9.85%
following the federal format of obtaining taxable
income almost exactly. The estate tax exemption was
just raised to $2 million for the next five years (until
2018). The marginal tax rates were reduced and now
range from 10% to 16%.

The corporate tax rate is a flat 9.8%. There also
are franchise taxes, and Minnesota has a specific S-
corp tax return, with minimum fees based on gross
assets within the state. More Minnesota tax
information can be found at: http://
www.revenue.state.mn.us/Pages/default.aspx.

Mississippi

A Mississippi resident who takes a job overseas

on a temporary assignment, travels extensively abroad, or leaves with the intention of returning, is still considered a resident. Personal tax rates fall between 3% and 5%. Most retirement income is tax exempt. Sales tax is 7%. There is no functional estate tax in Mississippi.

Corporate tax rates also range from 3% to 5%. It is important to note that if you owe over $200 on corporate tax, you are expected to make estimated payments. There is also a franchise tax computed on $2.50 of each $1,000 of capital employed and assessed value of property in your business, with a $25 minimum fee. More tax and business information can be found at: http://www.dor.ms.gov.

Missouri

A Missouri resident who moves abroad without maintaining a permanent abode in the state and visiting for less than 30 days each year can be considered a non-resident. Individual taxes span the distance from 1% to 6%, with the highest rate coming in at a grandiose $9,000. Social Security is mostly exempt, and a portion of some pensions are. There is no estate tax in Missouri.

Corporate tax rates are a flat 6.25%. Franchise taxes are only due if assets are over $1 million. The franchise tax, if due, is 1/150th of 1% (0.000067). For

more information, please see: http://
www.dor.mo.gov.

Montana

Montana residency status cannot be lost until residency in another state or country is gained. Tax rates range from 1% to 6.9% for individuals with the highest bracket coming in at $15,600. There is no estate tax.

Corporate tax rates are 6.75%. Personal service businesses, contractors, and lodging facilities have additional income taxes levied on them. More tax information can be found at: http://revenue.mt.gov.

Nebraska

Nebraska's rules for expatriates are remarkably strict. Nebraska residents moving abroad cannot relinquish their residency until they either:

1. Give up U.S. citizenship.

2. Establish residence as a permanent resident alien of another country.

3. Or, reestablish a permanent domicile in another state within the United States.

Individual taxpayers fall into tax brackets ranging from 2.56% to 6.84%, with the highest bracket coming in around $27,000. Social Security and pensions are taxable the same as how the federal taxes them. Nebraska's estate tax has been repealed.

Corporate tax rates range from 5.58% to 7.81%. In addition, an annual benefit report must be filed that costs $25 plus $5 per page for recording costs. For more information on business requirements, please visit: http://www.sos.ne.gov/dyindex.html for tax information: http://www.revenue.nebraska.gov/index.html.

Nevada

Nevada has no personal income tax and is thus a non-issue for expatriates. Nevada is also a good state for maintaining a mailing address, so as not to generate state tax letters when filing just federal returns as an expat.

There is no corporate tax in Nevada. There is, however, an annual list filing fee that ranges from $125 to $11,100 depending on the value of capitalized shares. Therefore, be sure to give your shares very low value if forming in Nevada. LLCs also pay a $125 annual filing fee for listing their member names. Both corporations and LLCs are subject to a $200 annual business license fee. While Nevada corporations are gaining popularity, Nevada likely leads the United States in LLC filings with its clearly written LLC laws. More information on business formation in Nevada can be found at: http://nvsos.gov/index.aspx?page=4.

Tax Tip: In states like Nevada and Delaware that charge and annual franchise tax based on share capitalization value, it pays off when forming the business to have a $0.001 or even $0.0001 share value. It also pays to have fewer shares issued.

New Hampshire

New Hampshire allows non-resident or part-year resident status only when the intent to remain abroad is permanent. New Hampshire only levies a tax on dividend and interest income—a flat 5% on any amount over $2,400. Not good news for S-corp owners in the state as most S-corp income is distributed as a dividend. There is no estate tax in New Hampshire.

Corporate tax rates are a flat 8.5%. Annual report fees for an LLC or corporation run $800. For more tax information, please see: http://www.revenue.nh.gov.

New Jersey

Under New Jersey law, a taxpayer may only have one domicile at a time. If the intent to stay in the new location is not permanent, then New Jersey residency has not been relinquished. Included as residents are also any individuals who maintain a New Jersey abode and spend greater than 183 days in the state during the tax year.

New Jersey tax rates range from 1.4% to 8.94% for individual filers. The top tax rate doesn't come into play until $500,000 of income is reached. Social Security is not taxable, but pensions are.

New Jersey has an inheritance tax—meaning if you are given or bequested real property worth more than $500, the state wants you to pay somewhere between 11% and 16% of the value to them. Ouch! New Jersey also has a separate estate tax on estates valued greater than $675,000.

New Jersey also charges a tax on partnerships, based on a per-partner fee. Corporate taxes are a flat 9% with a $500 minimum tax. More New Jersey tax information can be found at: http://www.state.nj.us/treasury/taxation/index.shtml.

New Mexico

New Mexico is another state where the intent to establish a permanent domicile in another location is what makes the relinquishment of residency allowable. If leaving with the intention of returning to the state, then residency is maintained. New Mexico is one of the states that can be tough about enforcing these provisions and the intent of the move must be proved by clear and convincing evidence, which is a high standard to meet.

Individual rates range from 1.7% to 4.9%. An inheritance may be included in modified adjusted gross income and taxed that way, but there is no specific inheritance or estate tax.

Corporate taxes range from 4.8% to 7.3%. Rather than a sales tax, New Mexico has a Gross Receipts Tax that, if you have a business of any type in the state, you must file returns at least bi-annually. More information on New Mexico taxes can be viewed at: http://www.tax.newmexico.gov.

New York

New York is another state that many people think is a difficult state to relinquish residence in, but for expats this is not the case as a safe harbor provision exists. If less than 450 days are spent in New York within any 548-day period and spouse and children are not present within the state for longer than 90 days each year, the person is not considered a resident of New York.

Often though, being a resident of NY is more tax beneficial than being treated as a nonresident. Unlike most states, NY levies taxes on nonresident employees of NY companies based on the company location, even without any work being done in-state, and the full amount is considered taxable. Whereas as a resident, employees who work in other states receive credit for state taxes paid on the same income. But for those who are nonresidents, there is no credit applied, creating double taxation of the same income.

Personal tax rates range from 4% to 8.82%. New York City also has an income tax. New York has an estate tax over $1 million if the decendant is a U.S. citizen, or if a non-citizen only if they need to file federal estate tax. Talk about trying to give people a reason to surrender citizenship!

Corporate tax in the big apple is a flat rate 7.1%. There are a range of business credits available as well—ranging from film credits to solar installation and more. For more information on NY taxes, you may view: http://www.tax.ny.gov.

North Carolina

Expats who leave from North Carolina have the burden of proving both that they have established a new domicile and that they have abandoned their domicile in North Carolina. While it is clear that anyone who spends more than 183 days in the state is considered a resident, it is not true on the flip side that being absent from the state for more than 183 days will establish non-residency.

North Carolina has a flat tax rate of 5.75%. The estate tax in North Carolina has been instituted and repealed several times. Currently there is no estate tax.

The corporate income tax rate is a flat 6.9%.

North Carolina also imposes a franchise tax of $1.50 per $1,000. For more information please see: http://www.dor.state.nc.us.

North Dakota

Residency in North Dakota is determined by living within the state for greater than seven months within the tax year and maintaining a domicile there. Residents moving in or out of the state are allowed part-year filing status.

Individual tax rates range from 1.22% to 3.22%. No estate tax is due regardless of the estate's value, but an estate tax return must be filed nonetheless.

Corporate taxes range from 1.48% to 4.53%, financial institutions are levied an additional tax. For additional information, you may view: http://www.nd.gov/tax.

Ohio

Ohio does not give a clear distinction of what it takes to give up residency. It makes determinations on a case-by-case basis using the following factors:

1. Number of contact points the individual has in Ohio.

2. Individual activities in tax years other than the current tax year.

3. Any other fact the tax commissioner deems

relevant.

Personal tax rates are between 0.587% and 5.421%. Social Security is exempt and pensioners receive some additional tax credits. There is no estate tax in Ohio.

Corporate income taxes were repealed, but many corporations are still subject to the Commercial Activities Tax based on gross receipts. For more information on this and other business taxes in Ohio, please see: http://www.tax.ohio.gov/commercial_activities.aspx.

Oklahoma

Defines non-resident status as an individual who, out of a 24-month period, has been absent from the United States for 550 days, is not present in the state for more than 90 days in a tax year, and whose spouse and children are not residing in the state for more than 180 days in the tax year.

Individual tax rates range from 0.5% to 5.25%, with the highest bracket coming in at $8,701. Oklahoma does not currently collect an estate tax.

Corporations are taxed at a flat 6%. Oklahoma also charges a franchise tax of $1.25 per every $1,000 of assets in the state. For more information please see: http://www.tax.ok.gov.

Oregon

Oregon's official definition of nonresident includes a "foreign nonresident," which means someone who meets either the criteria for the bona fide residence test or physical presence test of the Foreign Earned Income Exclusion.

Individual rates range from 5% to 9.90%. An estate tax applies to estates valued at $1 million or more.

Corporate tax rates range from 6.6% to 7.6%, with a minimum tax of $150. Oregon also has a personal property excise tax on businesses. For more information, please visit the Oregon Department of Revenue at: http://www.oregon.gov/dor/Pages/index.aspx.

Pennsylvania

To renounce residency in Pennsylvania, a taxpayer must:

1. Maintain no permanent place of abode in Pennsylvania during the tax year.

2. Maintain a permanent place of abode elsewhere during the year.

3. Spend no more than 30 days aggregate in Pennsylvania during the tax year.

With a 3.07% flat rate income tax, Pennsylvania is one of the lower taxed states income-wise. Pennsylvania has no estate tax, but it has an inheritance tax of 4.5% when property is passed from parents to children, 12% to siblings, and 15% to all other heirs.

Corporations are taxed at a flat 9.99% and the rules are rather straightforward. For more detailed information, please see: http://www.revenue.state.pa.us.

Rhode Island

Rhode Island bases residency on maintaining an abode there. If a residence is owned within the state for at least 183 days in the tax year, even if the taxpayers are domiciled elsewhere, they are considered full-year residents.

Tax rates have been lowered recently in Rhode Island, with the new top rate being 5.75%, and the lowest rate is 3.75%. Rhode Island charges an estate tax, the current exemption is $921,655 for 2014.

The corporate tax rate has also just been cut to 7%, down from 9%. This takes effect starting in the tax year January 1, 2015. The franchise tax has also recently been repealed. With all these changes, Rhode Island is in the process of making itself a much more business-friendly state. However, S-corps are still caught in the middle of the law changes with a $500 minimum tax. For more information, you may see: http://www.tax.state.ri.us.

South Carolina

South Carolina is one of the states that makes it difficult to move abroad and relinquish residency. They consider those who move out of the state still residents unless they have fully severed ties, and will hunt residents down the world over demanding tax due. South Carolina sets out clear criteria for an expat to meet in order to abandon residency. It must be shown that the individual:

1. Has become domiciled in a foreign country.

2. Is no longer domiciled in South Carolina.

3. Has severed all connections with South Carolina.

4. Clearly has demonstrated an intent to reside abroad permanently with no intention to return to South Carolina.

Taxes range from 3% to 5% for individuals. There is no estate tax in South Carolina.

Corporations pay a flat tax of 5%. Many valuable tax credits are available, including a credit for developing corporate headquarters in South Carolina, and an abandoned buildings revitalization credit. For more information on taxation, please see: http://www.sctax.org/default.htm.

South Dakota

There is no individual or corporate income tax

in South Dakota. There are no estate taxes. Talk about an easy expat state! For more information on forming South Dakota businesses, you may visit: https://sdsos.gov/business-services/default.aspx.

Tennessee

Tennessee imposes income tax on those who both are legally domiciled in the state and those who maintain a residence in Tennessee for more than six months.

Only dividends and interest are taxed in Tennessee—wages and other earned income are not. An inheritance tax ranges from 5.5% to 9.5% of the value of the inherited property.

There is a corporate flat tax rate of 6.5%. There is also a franchise tax that is rather complex to determine, as it taxes various assets at differing rates. For more information, please see: http://www.tn.gov/revenue.

Texas

Texas has no personal income tax. This makes it a great state for expats to have as their last state of residence, and can be a good state to have a post office box or mail service in. There is also no estate tax.

Corporations don't have a tax, per se. However, there is a rather complex franchise tax return that must be filed by all business entities—including partnerships, joint ventures, and single-member LLCs. For more information on who is taxed, please see: http://www.window.state.tx.us/taxinfo/franchise/faq_tax_ent.html.

Utah

Utah does not provide a definition of who an expatriate is, but they have not been known to be a difficult state to relinquish residency in. Individual taxpayers pay a flat rate tax of 5%. There is no estate tax in Utah.

Corporate taxes also fall under the very fairly meted out 5% flat tax. There is a minimum $100 tax, but this does not apply to S-corps. For more information, please visit: http://tax.utah.gov.

Vermont

Vermont is very generous about residency; they only consider individuals to be residents for the time they are residing or domiciled in the state, and only if the aggregate time is over 183 days. Individual tax rates range from 3.55% to 8.95%. Vermont has a tax on estates valued over $2.75 million.

Corporate tax rates range from 6% to 8.5%. There also is a business entity minimum tax of $250 that applies to Partnerships, LLCs, and S-corps. More information can be found at: http://www.state.vt.us/

tax/index.shtml.

Virginia

Virginia is a domiciliary state, meaning that unless substantial steps are taken to abandon residency, you will still be considered a resident of Virginia after moving abroad. They consider those who move out of the state still residents unless they have fully severed ties.

Personal tax rates range from 2% to 5.75%. There is no estate tax in Virginia. There is a flat 6% corporate tax. There are no minimum taxes, but the late-filing fees are extremely heavy ($200 per month for the first six months), so be sure in this state that you file extensions and returns on time. More information on taxation in Virginia can be found at: http://www.tax.virginia.gov/

Washington

Another excellent state for expats, there is no personal income tax in Washington. There is an estate tax with a $2 million exemption amount, though.

There is technically no corporate income tax in Washington. However, there is a Business and Occupation tax, which essentially is an income tax based on gross receipts rather than net. Tax rates can be found at: http://dor.wa.gov/Content/

FindTaxesAndRates/BAndOTax/BandOrates.aspx.

West Virginia

West Virginia defines a resident as someone domiciled in the state and/or spending an aggregate of greater than 183 days in the state during the tax year. Tax rates range from 3% to 6.5% for individuals. There is no estate tax in West Virginia.

Corporations are taxed at a flat rate of 6.5%. There is also a franchise tax that charges $0.55 per $100 of taxable capital with a minimum tax of $50. For more information, please see: http://www.wva.state.wv.us/wvtax/WestVirginiaStateTaxDepartment.aspx.

Wisconsin

Wisconsin defines residency as every natural person residing within the state. Non-residents must file returns if earning over $2,000 in state source income. Individual tax rates vary from 4.6% to 6.65%. There currently is no estate tax in Wisconsin.

Corporate tax rates are 7.9% flat. For more information, please see: http://revenue.wi.gov.

Wyoming

One of the most cryptocurrency friendly states, Wyoming has passed some excellent legislation to entice companies promoting ICOs to be based in the Big Sky State. There is also no personal or corporate income tax in Wyoming, no estate tax, and the formation costs are very reasonable. For more information on tax in Wyoming, you can go to: http://revenue.wyo.gov.

18. PRACTICALITIES

Although preparing your own tax return may be more complex than anyone with more than simple cryptocurrency investments would want to take on, and I generally would not recommend it, if you decide to go that route you will need to know how to handle this.

Contrary to the instructions that are published by the IRS, payments from foreign banks and made in foreign currency is accepted for paying tax obligations. However, paying in U.S. dollars from a domestic bank is preferred by the IRS and may take longer than 30 days for the payment to be processed. A few states have started accepting cryptocurrency payments for state tax obligations, but this has yet to be established for federal tax payments.

Foreign credit cards are accepted for online payments, as long as they are MasterCard or Visa. In addition, you may pay by wire transfer.

Delinquent Filers

If you haven't filed the tax returns or FBAR reports that you needed to file, it is better to correct these oversights as soon as possible.

If certain required forms have been left out of your return and you discover this after filing, you will need to file amended tax returns. If you are simply amending a tax return to add FATCA forms that were non-willfully omitted, you may file an amended return merely as a cover letter, and all the financial amounts do not need to be completed, assuming no dollar amounts in the return were changed.

If no dollar amounts are needed, the filing process is rather simple.

- You check the box at the top of the page to identify the year of the return.

- Complete name, address, and Social Security

number.

• Complete Box III to explain the changes.

Where to File

For most returns of taxpayers living outside the United States, the return will be mailed to a special office for processing this. You should always refer to the instructions to verify this, but this is the most common address for mailing expat tax returns:

Department of the Treasury
Internal Revenue Service Center
Austin, TX 73301-0215
USA

If using a courier mail service, then the mail should be sent to this address instead:

Internal Revenue Service
3651 S Interregional Hwy 35
Austin, TX 78741
USA

APPENDIX

Comparison of Form 8938 and FBAR Requirements (2015) http://www.irs.gov/Businesses/Comparison-of-Form-8938-and-FBAR-Requirements

Internal Revenue Manual (2015) *Part 20. Penalty and Interest, Chapter 1. Penalty Handbook, Section 9. International Penalties* Retrieved from https://www.irs.gov/irm/part20/irm_20-001-009.html

Internal Revenue Manual, Part 5. Collecting Process (2015) Retrieved from http://www.irs.gov/irm/part5/irm_05-021-004.html

Internal Revenue Service (2015) *Scholarships, Fellowship Grants, Grants and Tuition Reductions* Retrieved from http://www.irs.gov/publications/p970/ch01.html

Internal Revenue Service (2017)*Revocation or Denial of Passport in Case of Certain Unpaid Taxes*, Retrieved From: https://www.irs.gov/businesses/small-businesses-self-employed/revocation-or-denial-of-passport-in-case-of-certain-unpaid-taxes#certification

Internal Revenue Service (2015) *Tax Guide for Individuals With Income From U.S. Possessions* Retrieved from http://www.irs.gov/pub/irs-pdf/p570.pdf

Internal Revenue Service (January 13, 2015) *Publication 590-A, Contributions to Individual Retirement Arrangements (IRAs).* Department of the Treasury.

Internal Revenue Service (2015) *Instructions for Form 2555, Foreign Earned Income.* Department of the Treasury.

Internal Revenue Service (October 7, 2014) *Revenue Procedure 2014-55.* Department of the Treasury

Internal Revenue Service (2018), *Combat Zones Approved For Tax Benefits*, Retrieved From: https://www.irs.gov/uac/Combat-Zones

Internal Revenue Service (2017) *Tax Benefits for Education*, Retrieved From: http://www.irs.gov/publications/p970/ch01.html

Internal Revenue Service (2017) *Contributions to Individual Retirement Arrangements (IRAs)*, Retrieved From: http://www.irs.gov/pub/irs-pdf/p590a.pdf

Internal Revenue Service (2018) *Instructions for Form 1040x*, Retrieved From: http://www.irs.gov/pub/irs-pdf/i1040x.pdf

Julson v. Julson, 255 Iowa 301, 122 N.W. 2d 329, 331 (1963)

LB&I International Practice Service Concept Unit (2013) Retrieved from: https://www.irs.gov/pub/int_practice_units/JTOCUC_09_6_5_08.PDF

Marcus, Phyllis E. (December 11, 2001) *MEMORANDUM SCA-148501-01.* Department of the Treasury.

Summary of Allowances and Benefits for U.S.G. Civilians under the Department of State Standardized Regulations (DSSR), DOS web page, Retrieved from http://aoprals.state.gov/content.asp?content_id=134&&menu_id=78&menu_id=78.

United Nations Insurance Plans (2015) Retrieved from http://www.un.org/insurance/page/health-plans

United States Tax Court (1985) Crow v. Commissioner 85 T.C. 376, Retrieved From: thttp://www.leagle.com/decision/198546185utc376_1441/CROW%20v.%20COMMISSIONER

United States Tax Court (2016) Alfred S. Co. v. Commissioner, T.C. Memo 2016-19, Retrieved From: http://ustaxcourt.gov/UstcInOp/OpinionViewer.aspx?ID=10691

United States Tax Court (2016) Topsnik v. Commissioner 146 T.C. 1, Retrieved From: http://ustaxcourt.gov/UstcInOp/OpinionViewer.aspx?ID=10670

US Supreme Court, *Kent v. Dules,* 357 U.S. 116, 125 (1958)
US Supreme Court, *Weinstein v. Albright,* 261 F.3d 127, 139 (2d Cir. 2001)

Index

A

accrue, *26, 66*
adriatic, *28*
advisor, *14, 32*
Afghanistan, *28*
Africa, *34, 44*
airdrop, *144*
airspace, *28*
Albania, *28*
aliens, *154, 157*
allocation, *75-76*
allowances, *74, 233*
amnesty, *136, 167*
anonymity, *143*

anti-money laundering, *165*
appreciation, *51*
assets, *5, 25, 50, 84, 105, 122, 124, 130, 158, 160-161, 165, 168, 171, 177, 179*
attribution, *129, 132-133, 136*
Austin, *230*
Australia, *44, 65, 82, 84, 95, 114*
Austria, *44, 92, 114*
autonomous, *49-50*

B

Bahrain, *28*
Bangladesh, *44*
Barbados, *44*
Belgium, *24, 29, 44, 83, 114*
benchmark, *161*
Bermuda, *6*
billionaire, *235*
Binance, *166*
Bitbay, *166*
Bitcoin, *5, 38-39, 140, 156, 166*
blockchain, *5-7, 12, 119*
Bosnia, *28*
Brazil, *35*
Bulgaria, *44*

C

California, *68*
Canada, *44, 92, 114, 149*
carryover, *30, 63, 73, 75-76*
casualty loss, *101*

Cayman, *122, 124*
census, *236*
certification, *231*
charitable contributions, *98, 100-101*
Chile, *114*
China, *44*
citizenship, *5-6, 17-20, 67, 93, 147, 153, 157-159*
civilian, *27, 67*
Coinbase, *166*
collectibles, *86*
compensation, *160-161*
compliance, *7, 17, 19, 51, 174*
computer, *109-110*
conferences, *38*
Congress, *13, 52-53, 103, 157*
contractors, *27, 31, 60, 67, 111, 144*
contributions, *29-30, 60, 73-74, 81-83, 94-95, 100-101, 104, 232*
Croatia, *28*
crowdfunding, *139, 141*
crypto, *5-122, 124-180, 229-236*
cryptocurrencies, *5, 11, 37, 40, 80, 109, 141, 166*

cryptocurrency, *5, 7,*
11-12, 18, 37-40, 43, 46,
78, 81, 87, 91, 109,
140-141, 164-166, 229
currency, *38-40, 140, 171*
Cyprus, *44*
Czech Republic, *44, 114*

dividends, *43-44, 52, 54,*
56-57, 74, 76, 106,
121-122, 134, 143, 236
documentation, *19, 54, 62,*
64, 125, 131, 161
dollar, *99, 103, 121, 180,*
229, 235
dollars, *40, 84, 90, 119,*
135, 139, 160

D

decentralized, *49-50*
deductions, *97-99,*
101-103, 105-106, 117,
152, 159
deferral, *51, 85*
Delaware, *122*
Denmark, *44, 114*
dependency, *23*
development, *141-142, 147*
diplomats, *60*
disclosure, *175, 177,*
179-180
dispositions, *136*
distributions, *29, 44, 51,*
74, 83-84, 94-95, 130,
153, 162

E

Egypt, *28, 44, 92*
election, *20, 46, 51-52,*
54-55, 63, 116, 135,
150-151
employees, *30, 32, 59-60,*
83
employer, *29-30, 33, 60,*
73-75, 82-83, 94-95, 109,
168
entities, *84, 116, 120, 122,*
128-129, 134
entrepreneur, *109, 119*
equipment, *34*
equities, *151*
Estonia, *44*

Ether, *49*
Ethereum, *49-50, 140, 166*
Euros, *40*
examination, *32, 75, 143*
exclusion, *26, 30, 32-33,*
  35, 55, 59-68, 70-77, 85,
  87, 99, 104-105,
  111-113, 121-122
exemptions, *98, 151*
expat, *6-7, 29, 59-60, 64,*
  87, 99-100, 103-105, 230
expatriation, *152-153,*
  156-158, 160-162

F

FBAR, *175*
Finland, *44, 114*
fundraising, *43*
fungible, *141*

G

government, *22, 30-31,*
  38-39, 52-53, 60, 76,
  109, 113, 140, 158
Greece, *44, 114*
guidance, *78, 139, 142*

H

Hungary, *44*

I

Iceland, *44*
immigration, *147*
India, *44*
Indonesia, *44*
influencers, *144*
institutions, *103*
inversions, *14, 52*

investments, *37, 39, 41-43,*
45, 50, 53-54, 57, 76, 80,
84-87, 90-91, 95, 126,
139, 151, 153, 165-166,
235
Ireland, *44, 92, 114*
Israel, *28, 44, 92-93*
issuance, *5*
Italy, *34, 44, 92-93, 114*
itemized, *70, 78, 98-99,*
101-102, 106, 152
itemizing, *98, 102*

K

Kazakhstan, *44*
kickbacks, *134*
Korea, *44, 114*
Kraken, *166*
Kuwait, *28*
Kyrgyzstan, *28*

J

Jamaica, *44*
Japan, *44, 65, 114*
Jordan, *28*
jurisdictions, *6, 137*

L

Latvia, *44*
legislation, *6, 52-53, 64,*
165
liabilities, *68, 130*
limitations, *70-71, 81, 85,*
128, 179
Litecoin, *140*
Lithuania, *44*
logic, *61, 139, 169*
loopholes, *104, 120*
Luxembourg, *44, 114*

M

Macedonia, *28*
Malta, *6, 44*
marriage, *24-25, 34*
media, *6, 108, 174*
Mexico, *44, 149*
miners, *109*
miscellaneous, *101*
misinformation, *165*
Montenegro, *28*
Morocco, *44*

N

Netherlands, *29, 44, 83, 114*
New Zealand, *44, 84*
nodes, *110*
noncitizens, *151*
nonresident, *20, 22, 128, 153*
Norway, *7, 44, 114*
notary, *22*

O

obligations, *6, 147, 176, 229*
offshore, *119, 121, 175, 178, 180*
offshoring, *120*
organizations, *13, 32-33, 49-50*
overreport, *166-168, 170*

P

Pakistan, *28, 44*
passport, *17-18, 22, 156, 231*
payouts, *94*
penalties, *26, 51, 56, 66, 126-128, 131, 147, 164, 167-168, 175, 178-180, 232*
percentage, *56, 75, 84, 86, 98, 115, 129, 133, 168*
performance, *234*

Philippines, *28, 44*
platform, *141*
Poland, *44, 114*
Poloniex, *166*
Portugal, *44, 114*
possessions, *16-17, 231*
practitioners, *55*
presale, *141*
procedures, *14, 87, 136,*
168, 175-179
procurement, *140*
proofing, *109*
proprietorship, *112, 116*
pseudonymity, *147*

R

refund, *102-104*
refundable, *103-104*
reimbursement, *30-31, 70*
remit, *143*
renouncing, *6, 20, 159*
rental, *45*
reorganization, *130*
repatriation, *56, 136-137*
residency, *17-19, 25, 147,*

150, 158-160
restrictions, *17-18, 60-61,*
81
retirement, *29-30, 33, 53,*
80, 82, 84-87, 90-91, 94,
104, 180, 232, 236
revenue, *85, 141, 230-233*
revocation, *62-64, 231*
Robinhood, *166*
rollovers, *94*
Romania, *44, 92*

S

Samoa, *16*
Saudi Arabia, *28, 78*
scholarships, *33-35, 231*
self-directed IRA, *87*
self-employment, *62, 113*
Serbia, *28*
shareholders, *51, 130, 135*
signatory, *168-170*
Slovenia, *44*
software, *75, 109*
Somalia, *28*
spouses, *46, 53*
spreadsheet, *84*

startup, *126, 235*
stepchild, *23*
stimulus, *103*
stipends, *33, 35*
Streamlined Procedure,
  22, 167, 175-179
Subchapter-S, *134*
superannuation, *84*
Sweden, *44, 114*
Switzerland, *6, 24, 34-35,*
  44, 82, 92-93, 95, 114

T

tax evasion, *165*
tax havens, *122*
taxability, *29, 35*
teachers, *68, 149*
technology, *5-6, 12*
terminology, *15*
territories, *16, 178*
Thailand, *44*
theft, *101*
threshold, *46, 77, 167*
thresholds, *32, 105, 152,*
  166

token, *43, 50, 56, 85,*
  140-144, 147, 166
tokenizing, *140-141*
traders, *5*
transit, *69, 75*
treasury, *57, 168, 170-171,*
  180, 230, 232-234
treaties, *7, 14, 19, 56,*
  91-93, 112-113, 120, 152
treaty, *32-33, 43, 45-46,*
  57, 75-76, 92-93, 110,
  112-113, 121-122, 135,
  149, 151-152, 158, 162
Trinidad and Tobago, *44*
Tunisia, *44*

U

Ukraine, *44*
underpayment, *127*
underreporting, *164, 166*
unemployment, *74, 76, 97*
United Arab Emirates, *28,*
  59
unpaid taxes, *231*

V

visas, *20, 29, 149, 156*

W

wallet, *166*
wealth, *78*
wealthy individuals, *5, 50, 59, 165*
willful, *175-178, 180*
workers, *32, 61, 113, 149*
worthless, *25*

Y

Yemen, *28*
Yugoslavia, *28*

·

www.ingramcontent.com/pod-product-compliance
Lightning Source LLC
Chambersburg PA
CBHW060254220326
41598CB00027B/4094